THE JOL
KAMAU

Dawn N. Hicks Tafari, PhD

Dedication

This work is dedicated to my daughters, Dé and Niani. You inspire me to be a better human every day. I breathe because you live. Every good thing I do, I do to make you proud to call me your Mother.

This work is also dedicated to the blessed, sweet memory of my SistaFriend, Auset Siat Egun—LeeEster Niajallah Hendrix-Wilson—Iya Omi Ire. Tua-u for sharing your gifts with me. You pushed me to grow to heights I never imagined I could reach. I miss you.

THE JOURNEY OF KAMAU MILLER: HIPHOP COMPOSITE COUNTERSTORIES FOR BLACK MEN TEACHERS

Dawn N. Hicks Tafari, PhD

THE JOURNEY OF KAMAU MILLER: HIPHOP COMPOSITE COUNTERSTORIES FOR BLACK MEN TEACHERS

Copyright © 2023 by Universal Write Publications LLC

All rights reserved. Except as permitted by U.S. copyright law, no part of this work may be reproduced or distributed in any form or by any means, or stored in a database or retrieval system, or otherwise, without written permission from the publisher, except in the case of newspapers, magazines, and websites using quotations embodied in critical essays and reviews.

All third-party trademarks referenced or depicted herein are included solely for the purpose of illustration and are the property of their respective owners. Reference to these trademarks in no way indicates any relationship with, or endorsement by, the trademark owner.

Printed in the United States of America.

Mailing/Submissions:
Universal Write Publications, LLC
421 8th avenue, Suite 86
New York, NY 10116

Website: UWPBooks.com

Cover illustration by Anwar Wilson

ISBN: 978-1-942774-91-4

This book has been partially supported with a financial grant from SAGE Publishing.

Table of Contents

Acknowledgments	vii
Foreword by Dr. Marvin Lynn	xi
Preface	xv

Chapter 1: Just a Black Girl Minding Her Black Girl Business Out Here Crafting Composite Counterstories	1
Chapter 2: Tell Me About Yourself	7
Chapter 3: Back in the Days When I Was Young	21
Chapter 4: I Can't Hug the Kids	35
Chapter 5: You Don't Have to Wonder What My Motives Are	43
Chapter 6: Whose World is This?	59
Chapter 7: The Elementary School Was Where I Needed to Be	69
Chapter 8: I Decide What a Black Man is Every Day	83
Chapter 9: The Solution Has to Be a Collective Effort	101
Chapter 10: Inauguration Day	115

Epilogue: A Love Letter to Black Men Teachers	137
Afterword by Dr. Cheryl Matias:	
Every [Black] Boy Needs a Little Love	139
Pulling Back the Curtain	141
Appendix A: Interview Questions	143
Appendix B: Participants' Profile Chart	145
Appendix C: Answering My Research Questions	147
Appendix D: Looking Ahead: Implications for Future Research for Researchers	151
Appendix E: Resources for Black Men Teachers	155
Notes	171

Acknowledgments

I am the Mother of Dé Naṣara Tafari and Niani Gazi Elon Tafari.

I am the Daughter of Diane Miller and David Hicks, Jr.

I am the Granddaughter of Joan Blocker & Charles Miller & Edwin Wilson and Clara Barnett & David Hicks (Higgenbottem).

I am the Great-Granddaughter of Jessie Campbell & James Blocker, Ada Cox & Woodson Barnett, and Narcissus Charley & London Higgenbottem.

I am the Great-Great Granddaughter of Penolia & John Henry Campbell, Rachael & Frank Higgenbottem, Nancy Barnett & Anderson Thompson, Frances (Lucy) Allen & George Cox.

I am the Great-Great-Great Granddaughter of Cornelia, Sally & Alexander Cox, Dilsey Page & James Allen, Matilda Hackney & Samuel Barnett.

I am the Great-Great-Great-Great Granddaughter of Lucy & Foster Hackney.

My People are mighty, magical, and ever present! It is because of them, I live such a beautiful, blessed life filled with love, support, guidance, and divine intervention. *Mojuba Egun!*

I give thanks and praise to my Creator, Olodumare, for giving me breath. I only pray that I have done (and will continue to do) good things with this breath and that I have used my life to make others' lives better.

A girl from Edenwald Projects in the Bronx does not earn a PhD without the support of a Powerful "village." I must say that I am thoroughly blessed to have a community of family members and friends who love me, believe in me, and support me. I acknowledge that your love, faith, and support is a privilege; I am humbled and honored; and I will work, until I take my last breath, to continue to make you proud.

My Mother always knew that I would write a book one day. When I was a little girl, she would say, "One day, you're going to write a book about my life." Ma, thank you for seeing me before I saw myself. Thank you for believing that I could be great. I hope you enjoy this work. I love you.

Dad, your gentle spirit and generosity have made it impossible for me to ever not love men. ☺ Thank you for being such a light in my life. I love you.

I am thankful for my aunts Shirley Hicks Jackson and Deborah Hicks Johnson. Aunt Shirley, your loving support and ceaseless encouragement keeps me going. I can always feel your smile through the telephone. Aunt Deborah, you made the phone call that put in motion my career as an educator; I will never forget that. Thank you for your confidence in me and for always making me feel 10 feet tall.

Modupe pupo, Iyalosha Folami Oya'ayode R. Olopade-Abioye, for your love, guidance, support, and leadership throughout this process. This book could not happen until I aligned my professional self with my spiritual self. You have helped (and *are* helping) me to do that—gracefully, powerfully, and patiently. I am grateful for you. I am grateful for your Ashe. I say, "*Mojuba!*" to your Egun for placing you in my path. *Mojuba Iyalosha!*

Tiffany, my LoveBug, thank you for your patience, support, and love. When I thought I had hit a brick wall, you threw me a ladder and helped me climb over it. Thank you for brainstorming with me and for believing in me. I love and appreciate you.

Oyadara, JamillahNeeairah, Ankhi Ma'at, Dandara, and Wandee: our sisterhood is unmatched. You each inspire and motivate me in your uniquely amazing ways, and I am grateful to be able to call you my sisters. You remind me to keep my feet on the ground while soaring above the clouds. That kind of magic is only possible through the love of an incredible village of sisters.

My dear friend, Shaka Rawls. Our friendship of over 13 years continues to confirm that you are the epitome of passion, talent, and power. All Black men educators should know you. I'm glad that I can call you my friend.

Dr. Cheryl Matias, *mi amiga querida*. I truly do not know how I would have gotten through this process without you. You see the scholar in me that I've always dreamed of seeing, and you pushed me to actualize her. You inspire me above and beyond. Thank you.

I first learned about composite counterstories at the Critical Race Studies in Education Association conference where I attended a presentation by the brilliant Dr. Daniella A. Cook. Since then, she has become a mentor and a friend. Thank you for letting me walk and work with you. Sis, I appreciate you, and I see you.

I discovered Dr. Marvin Lynn's work on Black men educators when I was a doctoral student. I promptly read his dissertation and every one of his publications that I could get my doctoral student hands on. I learned so much from your scholarship. But I count myself especially blessed to have been able to get to know you as a person. Thank you for that free ride to the Philly airport back in 2012 ☺; I was fangirling big time, and you were incredibly kind and generous. I appreciate your time and your mentorship over the years.

I have had the honor of sharing space with some truly incredible scholars. Dr. Theodorea Berry, Dr. Denise Taliaferro-Baszile, Dr. Dave Stovall, Dr. Michael Jennings, Dr. Bettina Love: thank you for dropping jewels in my path and for walking the talk. Watching you and listening to you forced me to elevate my game. You have no idea how much I have learned from you. You are invaluable to the movement.

Mr. Craig Martin, you are a true inspiration. Your passion and focus are incomparable. I am grateful to have you in my space. I am even more grateful that children and their families get to have you in theirs. You have already positively impacted so many lives. I cannot wait to see what you do next!

When I handed in the Plan of Study for my dissertation, I told Dr. Leila Villaverde that I hoped I'd get an A on it, and we laughed at my zeal. Dr. Villaverde, my Doctoral Advisor and Dissertation Chair, you've never led me astray. You have been an ear and guiding light throughout my doctoral studies, my climb to Associate Professor, and this book acquisition. Thank you for staying only a text message away—no matter the time of day. I appreciate you.

Dr. Ayo Sekai, you are a giant. I did not think I was ready to write a book, but you proved me wrong. The work you are doing in the publishing industry is inspiring. Thank you for your enthusiastic support and compassionate guidance throughout this process.

Writing composite counterstories requires a sincere respect for and close attention to one's data. This is a creative process, but one must be mindful not to get so lost in creativity that you get too far from the stories that have been shared with you. I also honor that as a Black ciswoman, I must do my work with and about Black men honestly, carefully, and respectfully. Thus, over the years, I have accumulated a cadre of trusted consultants who answered my questions and helped to ensure I was authentically honoring Black male spaces. Thank you for your time, energy, and expertise: my beloved little brother, Mr. Greg E. Lynch, Jr.; my daughters' father, Dr. Nwachi Gamba Eze Tafari; my comrade, Mr. Shaka Rawls; and recent Leo High School graduate, Mr. Chris Mathis.

Nine Black men teachers informed this work. This work is possible because they were generous and courageous enough to trust me to tell their stories with integrity and authenticity. Thank you for your trust. Thank you for choosing education as your life's work. Our children are better, the field is better because of you.

Foreword

Marvin Lynn, PhD

Dean & Professor, University of Colorado Denver, School of Education & Human Development

In this book, Dr. Dawn Hicks Tafari—a critical race theorist, a lover of HipHop, and a scholar who studies the work and lives of Black male teachers—takes us on a journey to explore the life of Kamau Miller, a fictionalized character who is a composite of the many Black male teachers that she has studied over the years. The book, written in the style of Derrick Bell's chronicles *Faces at the Bottom of the Well* and *And We Are Not Saved*, allows us to listen in on the conversation between Dr. Tafari and Mr. Miller—an elementary school teacher. At times, the author is reflective about her own history, her positionality, and her intentions. At other times, she is interrogating some aspect of Mr. Miller's practice. In other ways, she takes note of the activity around her and reflects on it in important ways. The book is written in a conversational manner and generally avoids academic jargon. So, while the term "Critical Race Theory" is not explicitly used, it is in practice.

Dr. Tafari's work is, in one sense, groundbreaking. It draws on historical information—including accounts of qualitative interviews with Black male teachers, theoretical and conceptual literature on race, and documented evidence about the community in which Mr. Miller lives—to create a set of stories about this teacher that give us access to his thoughts about the world, his classroom, and the community where he lives and works. We also have access to Dr. Tafari's questions and wonderings about her work and the potential contribution she is making as she chooses Mr. Miller (a composite character) as her subject of interrogation and analysis. In the tradition of Bell, Solórzano, Yosso, and Daniella Cook, she creates a counterstory that is borne out of painstaking research on a critical reinterpretation of Black Education in the United States with HipHop as a context.

Dr. Tafari is courageous. She is choosing to do *this* work during a time when educators across the nation—but particularly in the south where she works and lives—are being persecuted for talking about race in the classroom. Teacher Educators are being symbolically indicted for having the gall to encourage preservice teachers and other emerging professionals to consider their own racial identities and attendant privilege as they pursue a career pathway that places them in the center of classrooms and communities that are not their own. Critical Race Theory has been named by many on the conservative right as the enemy. However, democracy—as we know it—is under attack. It's a political effort to constrain, restrict, and control free speech, freedom of self-expression, and workplace autonomy for educators at all levels. It is also an effort to overtly whiten the curriculum in ways that are ahistorical and dishonest. In short, Dr. Tafari's courageous efforts serve as an important counterweight to this movement. As a scholar and leader of a certain age who won't likely be crafting new studies or writing new books on these subjects, I take delight in knowing that younger scholars will continue the tradition of insurgent scholarship that powerfully speaks back to the White supremacist tradition within and outside of the academia.

I must say that I'm also pleased about Dr. Tafari's accessible approach to unwrapping and speaking back to White supremacy. Her counterstory could be accessible to those within and outside of academia in ways that make it even more powerful than typical scholarship like mine, that draws on academic jargon and requires folks to have preexisting knowledge about the theoretical concepts and methods we are using to build a legitimate case that is likely to be embraced by those in the academy. Bell's counterstories, for example, are written in a conversational style but the conversation takes place between two high-powered brilliant legal scholars. So, while it is a conversation—it is not one that is necessarily accessible to nonacademic audiences. In fact, while Bell's work was popular within the public realm—it likely began as a heuristic and a pedagogical tool for emerging legal scholars who were woefully underexposed to teachings about race in the United States. Because of the influence of HipHop—a discourse that was developed by and for Black and Brown communities in large urban enclaves like the Bronx in New York City—she chooses to use "plain English" in combination with Ebonics, at times, to communicate her ideas—big and small. This is a true feat during a time when it might be convenient for scholars to take the easy path of writing in a tradition that is inaccessible to folks outside of their field. It certainly would make it more difficult for conservative political pundits to try to use her work against her because they simply would not understand it. In this case, her work is accessible—even to severely undereducated conservative political pundits. So, there is risk involved. Dr. Tafari, though, in the tradition of Critical Race Theorists like Derrick Bell, Kimberlé Crenshaw, Daniel Solórzano, and Gloria Ladson-Billings is clearly not motivated by fear. Thank God.

The true blessing of this work is that it is also potentially accessible and usable to folks in underserved Black and Brown communities who can draw on the lessons learned from the dialogue between Mr. Miller and Dr. Tafari as a way to possibly transform the curriculum, reimagine how we teach Black and Brown children, find ways to better support and retain teachers of color, transform school financing to make it truly equitable, or consider the perspectives of teachers of color in education policy decisions at state and national levels. This work has the potential to be transformative on many levels. I am encouraged, inspired, and heartened by Dr. Tafari's courage and her commitment to tell our stories honestly and fearlessly. Schools, universities, and public libraries all over the country should enthusiastically adopt this work.

Preface

I need you to know that I am a Black girl from the Bronx—proudly, unapologetically. And I was raised in Edenwald Projects. Growing up in Edenwald made me resilient. I've seen things as a child that no child should see. In fact, I've seen things that no *person* should see: things like dead bodies, gunshot victims, and people smoking crack. However, the things that I have seen and the experiences I have had, laced with a HipHop soundtrack, all contributed to who I am, how I see the world, and how I navigate my humanity. My scholarship is one of the languages that my humanity speaks. And *this* book is the utterance of a long line of human beings who have walked in the world waiting to be seen as they are and not as someone else desires them to be.

The Journey of Kamau Miller: HipHop Composite Counterstories for Black Men Teachers has been in my spirit ever since I was a doctoral student studying Black men teachers. Inspired by bell hooks to create and share scholarship in a manner that is engaging, interesting, and accessible, I set about searching for my *way*: the way that I would conduct research, the way that I would write, the way that I would engage readers so that they were not bored to death. I first learned about Derrick A. Bell's *Faces at the Bottom of the Well* at a local conference in 2009. Then, in 2011, I found my way to the Critical Race Studies in Education Association annual conference at Teachers College in New York City. During that conference, I attended a workshop by Dr. Daniella A. Cook in which she shared her method for "writing CRT."[1] I was fascinated by the "unapologetic creativity"[2] and moved to embrace this incredibly empowering way of presenting research on, about, and with folk in marginalized communities. After that moment, I was never the same. I had found my way.

As mentioned, this book has been my heart's desire for a long time now. My goal has been to pen a compilation of composite counterstories that paid homage to the work of Derrick A. Bell, highlighted the lives of Black men teachers, and showcased the empowering impact of HipHop on all our lives. I birthed *Kamau Miller* in 2016. I created him as composite character in tribute to the nine amazing, Black men elementary school teachers who participated in a research study I conducted. His first name, Kamau, is Kikuyu[3] for "quiet warrior." Kamau is the name that I had chosen to give my first biological son, but I had two beautifully brilliant daughters instead, so it made perfect sense that I would give birth to Kamau on these pages. Kamau is special to me—so special that I also gave him my mother's maiden name (Miller) to round out his humanity. To further honor my family, especially those who've come before me, I've named all the other composite characters with whom Kamau interacts after my family members as well. This is in pure alignment with my love for this work and my respect for the legacy of which I am part.

The Journey of Kamau Miller takes place during one academic year in Mr. Miller's life: April 2022–June 2023. Each Composite Counterstory (CCS) takes place during a different part of the year, in a different location and incorporates different composite characters. Chapter 1: "Just a Black Girl Minding Her Black Girl Business Out Here Crafting Composite Counterstories" serves as the Introduction to this text. In this chapter, I share a bit more about who I am: a Bronx girl, a HipHop Baby, and a HipHop Feminist. I share how I first became a teacher, how I navigated New York City Public Schools as a new teacher, and how I developed my passion for Black men teachers. In this chapter, I also describe my process for raising Kamau and for developing composite counterstories. Chapter 1 sets the tone for the chapters to follow as this is a sharing of how my love for HipHop and teaching are intertwined.

In the first CCS, "Tell Me About Yourself," we meet Mr. Kamau Miller, a third-grade teacher from New York City, who lives and teaches at Derrick Bell Elementary School in the Hill District in Pittsburgh, PA. It's April of 2022, and he has agreed to participate in a research study being conducted by a doctoral student, but he's nervous. Consequently, he flips the script on her by taking on the interviewer role, compelling her to earn his trust and earn his story. The Black Feminist qualitative researcher, initially taken aback by the switch-up, promptly concedes. She bares her heart and shares her reason for conducting a study about Black men teachers and earns Kamau's trust. The third chapter of the text, "Back in the Days When I Was Young," takes place in June of 1999. In this flashback, we meet 15-year-old Kamau as he reconnects with his uncle and digs deeper into his relationship with his father during a casual game of basketball with the two older men. We also get an honest introduction to Kamau's hunger for learning and interest in all things education. Via Kamau's dad and uncle, we learn many of the life lessons the study's participants shared about their own childhood and upbringing.

In the fourth chapter and third CCS, "I Can't Hug the Kids," we meet Kamau's longtime friends, Adam and Terence, as the three friends interact with high-school senior Eric over a game of basketball at Rucker Park in Harlem, NY, during the 2022 Thanksgiving weekend. The composite characters in this CCS help to facilitate our understanding of the contradictions that arose during data collection around the concept of passion in the classroom. Is the elementary school classroom a safe place for a Black man to exhibit eros? Kamau and his friends take us on a journey through the souls and minds of nine Black men who are elementary school teachers who love what they do. In the fifth chapter and fourth CCS, "You Don't Have to Wonder What My Motives Are," we learn more about Kamau's wants and desires outside of the classroom. In December 2022, he attends a pre-Kwanzaa celebration with Diane, the cultured, intelligent woman he has been dating since April. This CCS incorporates data from the gentlemen's personal lives and provides another layer of humanity for Kamau by bringing us into his romantic world.

In the sixth chapter and fifth CCS, "Whose World is This?," Kamau Miller is preparing to kick off the 2023 Memorial Day Weekend with his friends when he meets Jerry Level, the owner of the barbershop, Levels, in Harlem. As Kamau is getting his hair cut, he is engaged in an empowered conversation about his experience working with Black boys versus how society often sees them. The data shared here speaks directly to the theme of "otherfathering"; and as the barbershop is known within Black culture as a safe, educative space, especially for Black men, their conversation runs the gamut from HipHop to education to the adultification and criminalization of Black boys. The seventh chapter and sixth CCS, "The Elementary School Was Where I Needed to Be," takes place a few hours after Kamau Miller's experience at Levels. He has joined his friends, Adam and Terence, at a Scotch & Cigars Party in the SoHo[4] area of Manhattan. During the party, the three longtime friends meet Mr. Foster Hackney, an insurance underwriter; and the four gentlemen become involved in a fascinating debate about the reasons Black men do not teach versus the reason they do.

The eighth chapter and seventh CCS in this text is "I Decide What a Black Man is Every Day." This CCS takes place at Derrick Bell Elementary School after the last PTA meeting of the 2022–2023 school year. This piece features Kamau Miller enthralled in a discussion with one of his student's parents and his student teacher about the upward battle that many Black male teachers face and some of the tangible ways they work to affect real change in today's schools. In the ninth chapter and eighth CCS, "The Solution Has to Be a Collective Effort," we join HipHop aficionado Kamau Miller on his travels to the Critical Race Studies in Education Annual Conference in June 2023. During a layover in the Atlanta airport, he meets and strikes up a conversation with a Black man teacher from North Carolina who does not share Kamau's love for HipHop, especially in the classroom. During their layover, the two gentlemen become immersed in a powerful conversation that incorporates data from the larger study about the gentlemen's perspectives on the evolution of HipHop, how (or if) HipHop should be integrated into the curriculum, and the importance of encouraging students' creativity.

Chapter 10, "Inauguration Day," is a fast forward 10 years into the future. It's Presidential Inauguration Day in the year 2033. Hill Harper has just taken the oath of office, and Kamau is living his best life. He is the principal of the school he loves. He is married to the woman of his dreams. He has a beautiful family and an inspiring staff of teachers committed to bettering their students' lives. Everything is perfect, or is it? *The Journey of Kamau Miller* closes with the Epilogue, "A Love Letter to Black Men Teachers." The final chapter serves to conclude the Kamau

Miller experience with an expression of love and support for Black men teachers everywhere. I have also included an Appendix for readers interested in learning more about the initial research study and looking for resources for Black men teachers.

This work is my heart and soul. I truly hope you enjoy it.

CHAPTER 1
Just a Black Girl Minding Her Black Girl Business Out Here Crafting Composite Counterstories

JUST A BLACK GIRL

This is the Royal MC

Counting 1, 2, 3

Spelling L-O-V-E

The Lover, that's me.

Shifting in full gear

Lend me your ear

Not a boo, but a cheer

Kween Bakardi is here

Female lyricist

Rap soloist

I'll do you like this

And I'll blow you a kiss

I'm Kween B also known as The Lover

I love 'em right

And you know there's no other
I'm Kween Bakardi
And The Lover am I
You don't need drugs
'cause my love will get you high!

These lyrics are part of a rap I wrote in 1987 called, "The Lover." I was 13 years old, and I had dreams of being a female emcee because I had something to say. The summer after my 13th birthday, I recorded "The Lover" for my amateur demo tape at my friend's cousin's house. It felt so good to hear myself on the boombox as I played my own songs. I felt on top of the world because I was a real part of the new, hot culture and music style that was taking over the world: HipHop. HipHop is the soundtrack to my life. I am a self-proclaimed Black girl, HipHop Feminist,[5] Educator, and MotherScholar[6] from the Bronx who discovered HipHop Feminism within the lyrics of SupaNature's "the Showstoppa" in 1985. Growing up in the Bronx as part of the HipHop generation has influenced everything I have ever done. Every move I have ever made feels like HipHop. I see HipHop in every bend of light. I can smell it as it wafts from the speakers. I can taste HipHop in my favorite songs of every genre. Scratches and verses reverberate through my eardrums as I draw connections between everyday experiences and HipHop lyrics. I hear HipHop in every story, every speech, every poem, every melody. I am HipHop—honestly, vulnerably, authentically, dynamically.

HipHop is always with me. One summer day in 1993, my friends and I were heading back to the Bronx from the City[7] on the 2 train. I stood in front of them strap-hanging, while they sat on the gray benches, and I entertained my friends by rapping the lyrics I had crafted 6 years earlier. As only the best homegirls would, they cheered me on, so I rapped for much of the ride. The train was fairly empty: it was just the four of us and a few other people that day. As the train neared the Allerton Avenue station, a light-skinned Black woman of about 30, stood up and approached me, "Have you ever read bell hooks?" she asked. I had never heard of bell hooks, let alone read her. "No," I responded. "You should read *Sisters of the Yam*. It's a good book," she declared. I thanked her and told her that I would check out her suggestion. And I did. A few weeks later, I found the book in a bookstore and read it cover to cover. Consequently, my life was, literally, changed forever. *Sisters of the Yam* gave me a vocabulary that seasoned my HipHop sensibility. Auntie bell taught me phrases like "white-supremacist capitalist patriarchy."[8] She exposed me to Black Feminism and a Black Feminist understanding that would catapult me onto a transcendent journey that included traveling the world and performing in HipHop music videos as a backup dancer. The truth is, if it weren't for *that* Sista suggesting I read *that* book in *that* moment, my life today would be very different. I would not have developed the nuanced, flavored, and layered interpretation of HipHop that I have today. And I definitely would not have approached teaching or scholarship in the way that I have.

My road to teaching and scholarship was paved by powerful Black humans. After college, I felt a strong desire to serve. I wanted to make the world better, but I wasn't sure exactly how to do it. That answer came in Fairfax, VA, at my Aunt Deborah's kitchen table. She was a teacher; and in our conversation, I shared that I had been thinking about teaching, and she said, "I was waiting for you to say that!" In her next breath, she picked up her white, corded kitchen wall phone and called her best friend, Sharon (who was one of the assistant principals (APs) at a K–8 public school in Brooklyn, NY), and scheduled my interview. And just like that, I had a job interview for a teaching position. I was offered one of two positions: a fourth-grade classroom or a sixth-grade classroom. I really had my sights set on the younger children, but *Auntie Sharon* encouraged me to take the upper-level class because that was directly under her supervision (she was the sixth–eighth-grade administrator). She assured me that if I took the sixth-grade position, then she would wrap her arms around me and mentor me, and I believed her! I knew the value of mentorship, so I accepted the position teaching sixth grade at that school, and my mind was blown. As an elementary school teacher, I learned so much about children ... and adults ... and curriculum ... and the system. In my public school, I saw far too many Black boys being pushed out of the classroom and far too few Black men leading classrooms. I did my best to not perpetuate the crisis effecting Black boys in schools by designing creative, multimodal, culturally responsive learning experiences instead of referring my students to special education. I worked closely with my mentor and developed relationships with master teachers and administrators to learn more about teaching and learning as processes and as institutions. I asked questions: I wanted to understand the social hierarchy, the bureaucracy, the injustices I witnessed. I needed to know why things were the way they were. I needed to know what I could do to make things better. I had so many questions ... so, so many questions.

MINDING HER BLACK GIRL BUSINESS

Though I had lots of questions, I also knew that not every question had a clear, definitive answer. Therefore, I decided to mind the business that I found important: social justice issues affecting other human beings. I believe that no forms of oppression fall outside of "the humanist commitments of Black feminist thought."[9] Thus, I do not commit myself only to issues impacting women because women are not the only people in pain right now; we are not the only ones dealing with a "metaphysical dilemma."[10] And I have a vested interest "in transforming oppressive Black expressions of manhood"[11] because these causes are *not* conflicting. I support Black boys and men in educational, social, and political settings because I empathize with their struggle. It is my business because we share the issue of being bound by multiple and competing systems of oppression.

Much of my business minding has helped me to come to the realization that I was a critical race theorist long before I knew what Critical Race Theory[12] was. It had always been my goal as an educator to prepare children to transcend their current social class and transform the "structural and cultural aspects of education that maintain subordinate and dominant racial positions in and out of the classroom"[13] by becoming critical, liberated thinkers. I recognized the barriers facing people of color as they maneuver through an evolving society and the sifting, sorting, and stratifying process that is the American education system. Therefore, I became and remain committed to challenging and working against said system. So you see: I get my passion for learning and writing about Black men teachers honestly. My desire to better serve Black boys led me to working to understand the barriers Black men faced in the teaching profession, the reasons why they teach despite said barriers, and to learn ways that Black women can more effectively support our Black men colleagues.

OUT HERE CRAFTING COMPOSITE COUNTERSTORIES

Passion is powerful and important, but it is not enough. I am adamant that my work be accessible to the very people who contribute to it and to those who love them (Auntie bell taught me that). This resolve and my passion for Critical Race Theory led me to begin exercising the "unapologetic creativity"[14] associated with weaving my research and data into composite counterstories. This is a creative process that will take you, my beloved reader, on a fun trip into the lives of nine Black men elementary school teachers through the eyes and experiences of Mr. Kamau Miller.[15,16] Kamau is a 38-year-old third-grade teacher approaching his fifth year of teaching. He is intelligent, approachable, thoughtful, talkative, inquisitive, kind, and passionate about teaching. Kamau is a complex, multi-layered yet simple man who embodies many of the characteristics of the nine men on whom he is based. He loves teaching, and he loves his students so much that he willingly engages others who show interest in his chosen profession.

My process for developing Kamau is interesting and inspired by the works of some brilliant Critical Race Theorists[17,18,19,20] who laid the groundwork for me to blur the boundaries[21] so unapologetically. African peoples are a storytelling people. Our stories have purpose and focus. Similarly, "counter-storytelling is different from fictional storytelling. We are not developing imaginary characters that engage in fictional scenarios."[22] Over the course of one academic year, I collected data from one-on-one interviews and a 4-week long Facebook focus group with these gentlemen and then, I transcribed, coded, and sorted my findings. Each CCS speaks to one of the streams of interview data collected from a larger study that emerged once the data was sorted into the *purposes* Black men elementary school teachers teach. Further, each CCS speaks directly to the four functions of the CCS as outlined in the article, *Critical*

Race Methodology: Counter-Storytelling as An Analytical Framework for Education Research.[23] As a way of paying homage to Derrick Bell, the father of Critical Race Theory, I incorporated his hometown (The Hill District in Pittsburgh, PA) and his name into these stories as the site where Kamau Miller, the main character, lives and teaches. Though the context of each CCS is fictional, the locations are real. I did this to remain close to reality and to help the reader connect and relate on a deeper level. You will find Kamau in different settings, interacting with different composite characters. The dialogue from the transcripts of the nine interviews have been interwoven into the speech and actions of the characters involved in each story. Therefore, when you hear each character speak, know that you are hearing the words of the incredibly courageous gentlemen who shared their amazing stories with me.

I no longer dream of being an emcee, but I do still have something to say. This compilation of HipHop composite counterstories is my "contribution to this jam."[24] It's my love letter to Black men teachers for doing the work that others don't think they should be doing. It's my tribute to those Black men who do the work that others don't believe they're capable of doing. It's my testimony to the joy that comes when Black men embrace their full humanity and curate the kind of empowering learning experiences that only Black men can create. I've designed this book to be "lyte as a rock"[25] because I want you to see these men and be changed. I hope that Kamau and the stories in this book will remind Black men who teach or are interested in teaching how incredibly important they are to the world.

We see you.

We appreciate you.

We support you.

CHAPTER 2
Tell Me About Yourself

"And Submit."

Kamau clicked the button on the online form. He shook his head, "What am I getting myself into?" he thought. As a Black man teacher, the only one in his school building and one of the few in his district, he enjoyed meeting and networking with other men teachers on sites like MenTeach. The site hosted tons of resources and highlighted the positive things men in education around the country were doing. It also had an e-newsletter—a place to access an incredible variety of information relevant to men teachers; the April e-newsletter is where he saw the flier by this doctoral student at a university in North Carolina doing her dissertation research on Black men elementary school teachers from the HipHop generation. It said that men born between 1965 and 1984 were eligible. He was born in 1984, so he just made the cut. Her flier was accompanied by a photo, so he could see that she was a brown-skinned sista[26] with locs. She reminded him of his own sister, so he responded affirmatively, but he was leery about agreeing to participate in a "study." Questions filled his head, "What exactly is she 'studying'? What does she want to know? What kinds of questions is she going to ask me? I hope she doesn't try to get too personal; I don't like everyone in my business. Wait … will my homeboys and my colleagues know that I'm participating in a *study*? Ugh. I got too many questions. Why did I agree to do this?" Kamau sighed and sat back in his burgundy desk chair, folded his arms, and tapped his right foot. He looked around his classroom. He had painted the walls this past summer in alternating light hues of orange and blue—an ode to his hometown basketball team, the New York Knicks. He looked at the orange wall, the blue wall, the orange, the blue and was pleased. His students loved their colorful classroom, and they enjoyed creating charts and art to hang on the walls and from the ceiling. It was the coolest room in the building. He looked up at the process charts hanging from clothing wire draped from wall to wall and the student-made multiplication chart on the wall opposite his desk. He scanned the 26 student desks and chairs scattered around the room. Then, he looked at the photograph of his class on his laptop screen. He hoped they each got home okay and were getting their homework done. He thought about his own plans for the evening—lesson planning and dinner with Diane, a beautiful sista he had been dating for the last few weeks. They had met online, and he remembered being so anxious when he first reached out to her. He was feeling a similar anxiety in his belly now. He wondered if the doctoral sista would even respond. He sat up, leaned forward with his hands on his knees, and thought, "Can I recall my response?" He sighed and looked out the window.

In that moment, Jay-Z's "Big Pimpin"[27] came into his head, and he hummed the tune, tapping his hands on his knees. In that song, he felt that Jay-Z was speaking about attaining success and not being afraid to show it off. The song always inspired him and got him hyped whenever he was feeling nervous about something that he was about to do. His favorite line was "I got no patience, and I hate waiting." The line was antithetical to how he was as a teacher but spot on when he thought about who he was as a person. When he set his mind to doing a thing, he wanted it to happen immediately, but he also knew better. He straightened up. "It's all good," he said aloud. Tentative as he was, he was also intrigued. He thought it was cool that someone, especially a woman—a BLACK woman, was interested in learning more about Black men teachers, and this was an opportunity for him to be part of the bigger picture. Teaching is his heart's desire, and the world needs to know what incredible teachers Black men are and can be. In that vein, he took a deep breath. "Patience is a virtue," he reminded himself.

Just then, he heard the beep of an email notification. It ... was ... *her* ... the sista doing the study. She responded fast: she would be in NYC the last week of April and was asking if he'd be available to meet. Kamau smiled, nodded, and stated aloud, "Oh, Sis ain't playin'. Ahhight. I see you, Ms. Future Doctor." He replied to her email. He thanked her for doing this work and being interested in his story. He thanked her for being interested in Black men as educators. He checked his calendar and then suggested they meet for the interview on April 27th at 3:30 p.m. in his classroom. That would give him time to dismiss his class and get settled before she arrived. She agreed.

Over the next couple of weeks, Kamau watched the calendar as the days passed slowly. April 27th couldn't come fast enough. Being a teacher kept Kamau busy—between lesson planning, managing his students' quirks, teaching, and attending his students' extracurricular activities, he was looking forward to sitting down and talking with someone who was not a teacher or a parent about a topic other than the third-grade curriculum or Mikhail's behavior that day. But today was the day. He wasn't sure why he was so excited, but he was. After dismissing his class, he straightened the desks in his classroom, wiped the Essential Question and math lesson notes off the board, and sat down at his desk to eat a few of the strawberries he had left over from lunch before she arrived. This was the first time he had been able to sit down since lunch, and as on most days, he was beat. As he ate his strawberries, he thought about Diane. She was on a cruise with her homegirls, so he knew he wouldn't be hearing from her for another few days. He was enjoying getting to know her, and they were getting closer but taking it slow. He checked his phone for missed calls and texts and scrolled social media for any life-changing updates. Just then, he noticed a letter on his desk. He had almost forgotten that one of his students had brought him a letter from the front office just after lunch. He was in the middle of his math lesson, so he had told her to leave it on his desk. He opened the large manila envelope: it was addressed to him with the school address. Inside was a smaller, white envelope with "From Your Sister in Harlem" written in cursive on the front. He laughed to himself; he knew his sister was old school but sending a letter via snail mail ... to the school ... was a first. He popped another strawberry in his mouth and began to rip open the envelope. He heard a knock on his classroom door.

"Greetings! Mr. Miller?" A brown-skinned woman wearing black-framed glasses with long dark brown locs pulled back into a ponytail peeked into the classroom through the open door.

Kamau smiled and stood up from his desk, "Ms. Tafari? Come in please. Water?" Kamau held up a bottle of water and motioned for her to sit at any of the desks.

"Indeed. Thank you," she said through a smile, "I'm Dawn Hicks Tafari. Thank you very, very much for fitting me into your schedule. I know you have a lot to do, especially this time of year, trying to wind down."

"My time is your time. I'm free now." Kamau responded walking toward the center of the classroom.

Dawn smiled and sat down at the desk with the name "Niani Pressley" written on the name tag. As she reached into her bag and pulled out a notebook, pen, and small recorder, she looked around the room, "I love your classroom. Colorful and inviting!"

Kamau sat at Nasara Shaw's desk, the one closest to where Dawn sat, placed the bottle of water on Niani's desk, and grinned, "Thank you! My kids help me decorate it."

Dawn replied, "Thanks for the water. I love that you have engaged your students in the decoration of their classroom. That's really cool. How has your day been?"

Kamau responded that his day had been busy put positively productive. The entire third–fifth grades were steadily preparing for end-of-grade tests (EOGs), so this time of year could be stressful. The two scholars chatted for a few minutes about the stresses of teaching third grade because of testing requirements. They also shared the joys of teaching children at that stage in their development. "They keep me on my toes: always ready!" Kamau said laughing but very serious.

Dawn laughed with Kamau, simultaneously shaking her head up and down and side-to-side in agreement. "Whew," she took a deep breath, remembering her reason for being there, "thank you for that laugh, Mr. Miller. I'm sure you have lots to do, so we better get started. Do you mind if I record our conversation for accuracy?"

Kamau responded, "Absolutely not. No problem."

"Awesome. I'll also be taking some notes by hand," Dawn stated. She opened her notebook, turned to a blank sheet of lined paper, picked up her pen, and pressed the record button on her recorder. "So … Mr. Miller, tell me about yourself."

Kamau leaned back in the student chair and said, "Sure." Then, he stopped. The tentativeness was starting to creep back in. He didn't want to waste her time, but he needed a little more assurance before he shared his story. He asked, "I will, but tell me more about you first. Why is this sista studying Black men instead of Black women?"

Dawn was surprised by Kamau's question but pleased by his interest. This was not the first time she had been asked this question, but this time the context was different. She came to interview *him*, but he flipped the script on her! She laughed to herself. "Okay, I see you, Mr. Miller. You're gonna make me work for this interview, huh?" she thought. Realizing that her stance as a HipHop feminist and critical race researcher compelled her to be fully, authentically present during this process, she looked Kamau in the eye and began to share.

"Do you remember the artist, Leschea?" Kamau nodded, and Dawn continued, "In 1996, she sang the words *HipHop, HipHop is more than just music to me*. Her words resonated with me then and resonate with me today because HipHop is absolutely more than just music to me. I have always loved HipHop culture; I have always loved the music that signifies 'my people'—young people, Black people, people from the inner city, and people born between 1965 and 1984.[28] But I had no choice in this love affair. You feel me? HipHop chose me. I was born in 1974, and its music, art, and language are the foundation of everything I know. The first record I ever bought was Salt n' Pepa's 'The Showstoppa.' I paid three whole dollars for it in 1985, and I loved that song because of how these sistas straight up dissed Slick Rick and Doug E. Fresh. I saw Salt n' Pepa as two strong women who weren't taking any *mess* from these dudes. They even had a girl deejay! I felt so empowered. And that made me a HipHop feminist way back then. I was able to look past instances of misogyny in some HipHop music just as children are able to still love their drug-addicted parents. HipHop is so much more than just music to me; it is my culture; it reared me. I am HipHop."

Kamau nodded his head, "That's wassup, Ms. Future Doctor!"

"Yeah," Dawn continued, "And HipHop is also a pathway for me to better understand many of the Black men around whom I was raised and/or have come to know in one way or another. Most of the Black men who I know and love (my ex-husband, my brother, my cousins, my friends, my students) have experienced intense relationships with HipHop. For instance, my ex-husband grew up with the members of Leaders of the New School and drove them to the studio to record their first album; my brother has been working as a promoter for HipHop clubs and individual artists since 2003; and several of my male cousins are budding HipHop artists who travel the country performing. Through HipHop, many of the Black men I know feel free to express themselves and make their voices heard. And through HipHop, I can often hear a Black man's pain, his frustration, his love, his passion, his fury, and his desire. From songs like *The Message*[29]—'Don't push me 'cause I'm close to the edge. I'm trying not to lose my head!', to Common's *The Corner*,[30] in which he tells us that 'we write songs about wrong 'cause it's hard to see right', my brothas have been crying out for a long time." Dawn shrugs, "And I just feel like it's about time we start listening."

"I appreciate that, Sis," Kamau nodded, "I really do. So you taught third grade, right. Any other grades? What was your experience like?"

Dawn shook her head and took a sip of water. She wasn't expecting to be interviewed by her interviewee today, but she had time. She put the water bottle down and relaxed into the small chair. She recalled her experience teaching in Brooklyn, "My first year as a teacher was teaching sixth grade in Brooklyn. I had a boy in my class—he was Black and Puerto Rican—named Rick. Rick was in foster care—had been for some time—and oozed with wit and personality. He was charming and intelligent. He was also quite rambunctious," she laughed, "often ending up in trouble. As Rick's teacher, I was almost always pleased by his academic performance: he completed his assignments quickly and skillfully. However, once he was finished, he would set in harassing the other students, getting out of his seat, and being disruptive. I would move Rick's seat around the room in an effort to find the least distracting placement, but Rick had a way about getting his way. For example, when the Yankees swept the Mets winning the Subway Series, he harassed me until I unwillingly conceded to his demonstration of what the Yankees had done: this boy ran around that classroom with my broom saying, 'This is what the Yankees did! THEY SWEEEEEPPPPPPTTT THE METS!'"

Kamau laughed out loud. "Yeah, I've had a student just like that! So how'd you handle that?"

"Well," Dawn continued, "My frustrations grew with Rick's behavior, but I never referred him for special ed or recommended him for in- or out-of school suspension as some of my colleagues had suggested because I knew that he had been institutionalized since he was a young boy and that more institutionalization was not what he needed to achieve success. What I believed he needed was a break, a second chance at moving up the social pyramid, so I took on Rick that year, matching his misbehavior with my own brand of cool discipline. I took him to the homecoming football game at my alma mater, Hofstra, to show him that college was within his reach."

"Wow, that's wassup." Kamau said. "You guys still in touch?"

"Not at first. I got married and moved to Maryland, and he was moved to another home, so I lost touch with him. Nonetheless, he always stayed on my mind and in my heart, and I wondered for years how his life turned out. Did other teachers try to understand him as I did? Did they label him as a problem? Adultify him? Criminalize him? And lo and behold, my questions were answered just a few months ago: Rick actually friended me on Facebook! When I tell you I cried tears of joy as I looked at his college graduation picture with his *mom and dad*. I continued to cry when I heard his voice on the telephone, and he told me that his mom and dad adopted him when he was *sixteen*. And I cried even more when he told me how *I changed his life*. He said, 'You were the first person to ever tell me I could go to college'. He also told me that he had one Black man teacher in middle school who was also 'really cool'."

"Look at that!" Kamau sat up and pointed in the air as if pointing out the fact that a Black man teacher had positively impacted my student's life.

"Aw man. It's wild." Dawn asserted. She continued, "And he was blessed to get adopted by two wonderful people who gave him lots of love, paid for him to earn a Bachelor's and a Master's degree at top-notch universities. But, I always wonder where he would be today if I had not told him that he was smart enough to succeed in college, or if I had followed my colleagues' advice and referred him for special ed. I wonder what Rick would have done with his time if I had him sent home to his foster parents on suspension. Would he have still ended up in college at 18, or on Rikers Island?"

Kamau frowned and shook his head in acknowledgment of Dawn's implication.

"Thankfully, I will never know the answer to that question," Dawn responded, "But what I do now know, based on my conversation with him, is that my refusal to flow with the status quo and take the path that would have made *my life* easier year, made his life better. And isn't that what it's all about?" She took a sip of water.

"That's absolutely what it's all about, Sis!" Kamau answered. He was happy that he thought to engage the researcher in this way. Getting to know her heart was helping him feel more comfortable about sharing his story with her. He wanted to know more. "Have you seen this issue show up on a larger scale?"

She looked down at the desk and moved her water bottle from the left to right. She thought about her experiences as a former elementary school teacher, community college faculty, and current teacher educator at an HBCU.[31] She explained, "I work with all kinds of human beings on a daily basis. One of the things that I have consistently witnessed throughout my career as an educator has been the maltreatment and misfortune of Black males within the public education sector, and this maltreatment and misfortune is, and has been for a long time now, at crisis level. I don't need to tell you: there is a crisis affecting Black boys in public schools. They're referred for out-of-school suspension and special ed services at higher rates than any other group, and they have lower high school graduation rates than their white counterparts. In fact, much of the research on Black male success in public schools sheds light on the significant opportunity gap between Black boys and their white counterparts in reading and mathematics in more than 40 states."[32] She moved the bottle from right to left and shook her head, then said aloud, "This is a serious problem, and I can see and hear instances of this pain in HipHop music and reflected in how our babies behave."

Dawn looked at Kamau, who was looking at her as if he were waiting for her to continue. She declared, "Now I know the opportunity gap is measured using standardized testing methods that focus on a very narrow scope of *traditional* intellect. There are several avenues that can be taken to rectify this crisis. One of the ways that we may be able to help diminish these gender and racial disparities is by immersing Black boys in an educational environment in which they have realistic role models who share some of their cultural experiences and value their cultural capital, like you." She looked Kamau in the eyes. He was listening intently and biting his bottom lip. She felt her eyes welling up with tears, so she took a breath. This work was so important to her, but she did not want to seem overly emotional in Mr. Miller's classroom, so she took another breath, and continued, "*Effective* Black men teachers like you can serve as real-life role models—walking counter-narratives[33]—for the boys you teach and with whom you interact on a daily basis. Your presence matters."

Kamau could see the passion in Dawn's eyes. He could hear it in her voice, and he was grateful. As he sat there listening to her, all his doubt and anxiety melted away. He had no idea that this afternoon would turn into such a powerful learning experience for him. He asked, "What kind of impact do you think I, and men like me, have on our female students?"

Glad he asked that question, Dawn sat back in the chair and shared her thoughts, "All children are better off when they are exposed to a variety of educators, mentors, and role models. In 1999, this reporter named Joan Morgan wrote a book called *When Chicken Heads Come Home to Roost*,[34] and in it she talked about the importance of Black male figures in the lives of Black girls. She reminded us that many of us in the HipHop generation are the products of that one-out-of-two divorce rate. Too many girls have had violence, imprisonment, illness, addiction, depression, or abandonment rob them of fathers—both physically and emotionally. Yeah," Dawn shook her head, "Too little attention is paid to the incredibly significant role Black men play in shaping of their daughters' ideas about themselves, others, and love as a whole. All children can benefit from the existence of positive Black male figures in their lives—whether at home or at school. And because children spend many of their waking hours in school, those who do not have positive Black men in their lives at home may benefit from that presence at school—especially during the crucial developmental stages that occur during the elementary years."

"Absolutely!" Kamau cheered. "I know that there's too few of us. I read an article on the MenTeach website that said that about 16% of elementary school teachers are men. Less than 2 percent are actually Black men."

"Facts, Mr. Miller, pure fact," Dawn started. She was so excited to be engaged in this conversation with Kamau. "I began this research with the desire to amplify the voice of the minority: Black men elementary school teachers from the HipHop generation. I sought to uncover some of the reasons why—in spite of the low pay, minimal opportunities to supplement income, cultural implications stemming from, what we call, *the feminization of teaching*, and the profession's low status—Black men from this generation do teach on the elementary school level. That is why I'm here."

Kamau sat back in his chair. Dawn had given him much to think about. She was answering his questions as if she were in his head, and he was loving every second. He felt much more confident about who she was and what she might do with his story. However, her answers had led to more questions. She was giving him so much food for thought, but he was still hungry, so he picked up his metaphorical shovel and dug a bit deeper, "You mentioned becoming a Feminist when you were young, and then you said that teaching was feminized. I think I know what you mean, but I want to be sure. Can you talk about that a little bit?"

"Absolutely," Dawn nodded. This interview was turning out to be a complete switcheroo but she was cool with it. She shared, "Have you ever heard of Ntozake Shange? She wrote a book length poem called, *for colored girls who have considered suicide/when the rainbow is enuf*."

Kamau thought for a second, then said, "Yeah. They made a movie of it, right? Janet Jackson was in it?" He smiled and raised his right eyebrow. He's loved Janet Jackson since the first time he saw her.

"Yup. That's it," Dawn answered, "and in that poem, there's a moment when the Lady in Yellow says, 'being alive & being a woman & bein colored is a metaphysical dilemma I haven't conquered yet. Do you see the point? My spirit is too ancient to understand the separation of soul & gender'.[35] So stay with me for a moment. I promise I'm getting to the point." Dawn smiled at Kamau, took a sip of water, and continued, "She is speaking of the web of intersecting identities," Dawn linked her fingers together to demonstrate a web, "in which Black women are caught and often find themselves struggling to escape. Her humanity, her gender, *and* her race are intersecting identities—all of equal importance. She cannot separate them. One is not more important than the other. Their intersection is so powerfully inseparable that it causes somewhat of a problem for her because she cannot figure out how to conquer, or manage, said intersection. However, she concedes that this dilemma is incomprehensible … right?— She can't even understand it—because her soul and her gender have always been intertwined. So, there is almost no telling them apart, for each individual strand of her being is too much a part of her natural wholeness as a human to separate. You with me?"

Kamau nodded, "I'm with you, and I hear you. This race versus gender argument is a complicated issue. You feel like feminism helps? Real question."

"Indeed, it does. I mean, the irony in that inquiry is exactly why it makes such good sense. In other words, a *Black* Feminist approach allows me to work the contradictions that some may perceive of a Black woman studying Black men. Black Feminism is NOT a battle to take rights back from men; it is not solely a struggle for the rights of women; it is a way of uncovering how the human body is affected by power. It is the fight against said power and for the needs of those affected bodies, or groups of people, who have been historically ignored. Black Feminism helps because the body is not only gendered; it is also racialized. These two factors (along with sexual orientation, religious preference, etc.) color how one sees the world. My work as a Black feminist cannot be contained in a neat category. I am concerned for Black boys and men because their gender, compacted by their race, marginalizes them in a school system in which the majority of teachers are white, middle-class women. This lack of cultural congruence causes an imbalance in American schools as Black boys struggle—as *you* know—for survival and equitable treatment in—and outside of schools. You see, I am a warrior driven by the belief that no oppressions fall outside of the humanist project."

"Okay, Sis, so this is real for you?" Kamau sat forward in his chair.

"My agenda is clear; this work is personal." Dawn started. "I watched my brother struggle in school—as he tried to navigate the educational system's frequent suspensions and special education referrals with a very loose, somewhat non-existent support system. I do this mostly for him. However, when I became an elementary school teacher in Brooklyn, I witnessed firsthand how Black boys were overrepresented in the dean's office. Most teachers struggled with them; I struggled with them, yet I was intrigued—concerned for the light that I saw inside them that seemed to go unnoticed by most others. Black boys like Rick are another reason why this is so real for me. I mean, even though I could show Rick all the love in the world, I could feel in my bones that he also needed a male walking counter-narrative in his life. Perhaps, if my brother had had a strong, caring, and supportive male presence in school (as he did not have a male of this sort at home), then he would have graduated from high school. Perhaps, if my cousins Edwin and Samuel had had good Black men teachers, then they would not have dropped out of high school. Now, I'm not trying to say that all Black male academic progress is based on the presence of Black male role models, but I do believe that these consistent, positive interactions can improve academic success and make schooling a better experience for them all around. Throughout my 13 years of experience as a public school teacher and as a teacher trainer, I have known two Black male elementary school *classroom* teachers. And I can't help but wonder about the connection between the skewed numbers of Black boys in special education and out-of-school suspension and the low number of Black men teachers, especially in the elementary schools."

"Ahhh," Kamau started, "I was going to ask you why you were focusing on us men teachers in the elementary school."

Dawn smiled. "Yeah, I cannot ignore the issues facing Black boys and men today in elementary schools. Some may feel like these issues do not directly affect me, but I disagree: I have a father, a brother, a nephew, numerous cousins, and friends … who are all Black males. And even if I did not have these close relations with Black men, these serious discrepancies would still concern me. The gender imbalance in the teaching force is one consequence of these inequities. I mean, it's just a matter of fact: if Black boys do not graduate from high school or earn a GED, then they cannot graduate from college. If they do not graduate from college, then they cannot become teachers. And we need more Black men teachers. This work that I'm doing, Mr. Miller, is an opportunity for me to collaborate with those who are also affected by the imbalance … *and* care to do something about it. I mean, if I want to know why Black men become elementary school teachers, who else should I ask? No one can tell me about the Black male experience better than Black men." She shrugged and looked around the room. She could tell that he was tentative when she first arrived and could feel the tension melting. She hoped that he felt he could trust her with his story. She valued his humanity, and she would honor the words he shared with her.

Kamau placed both his hands on his thighs and leaned forward. He looked at Dawn and saw her passion. He was pleased. He was confident. He felt good about who she was and why she was there. He saw the question in her eyes, and he responded aloud. "I trust you. Thank you." He looked at the clock on the back wall of his classroom. Its hands reported 4:17 p.m. as the time. Wow, time has flown. He was loving this conversation, loving learning about her work and her ideas, but he figured he'd better stop acting like *he* was the one doing a dissertation. He sat back, opened his water bottle, and took a sip. He swallowed a few gulps of water and then took a deep breath. "What questions do you have for me?"

CHAPTER 3
Back in the Days When I Was Young

Back in the days when I was young, I'm not a kid anymore, but some days I sit and wish I was a kid again.[36] Ahmad's words swirled in Sean's head as the music played from a car in a nearby parking lot. Sean rapped along, then stopped, and looked up at the basket. "Whew! If I knew then what I know now," he said as he dribbled the basketball with his right hand.

He continued, "As the father of a 15-year-old male, I give it to him straight with no chaser. Just yesterday, we were playing ball and he could not hit a 3-point shot to save his life," Sean chuckled. "I immediately asked him why he did not drive the ball closer and take a more sensible shot. With his NBA Live 2000 mind, he says that he thought it would be easier to hit those long-range shots. My response was measured—even though I wanted to clock him in the chest, ya know like how Dad did to us to stop that urge? I told him that games always make things seem easier than they really are, but that it takes practice and skill to hit a 30-foot jumper. I told him that technology is great, but true skill comes from actually doing the work both mentally and physically." Sean stated as he tossed the basketball to his older brother. The two brothers always played a game of one-on-one when Dez came to visit. This has been their ritual since Sean graduated college, and they promised to continue it after Sean became a wheelchair user.

Dez dropped his duffle bag, caught the ball, and took a shot. He had called when he was getting off the highway, and his brother was waiting for him on the basketball court in front of the building he lived in with his family. This time with his little brother was valuable to him, but even more valuable was the opportunity to learn more about how his nephew, Kamau, was navigating high school. "So what he say?" He missed the basket.

Sean scoffed, "Needless to say, he got frustrated, but I had to keep him focused and concentrating on the goal at hand. I told him, *if you want to get better at shooting, you have to learn the fundamentals that a video game cannot teach you.* Currently, he is on video game restriction until I see the same commitment on the court that he puts into video games." He dribbled the ball with his left hand as he moved his wheelchair around the court with his right hand.

"Funny you say that because since my nephew will be staying with me for the rest of the summer, now I have a reason to make him come with me to the gym everyday." Dez took a jump shot. "Last time he and I played together, he would not come in and do a lay-up nor try to hit a free throw. It was so funny." He caught his own rebound and dribbled the ball. "We'll get some regular practice in."

Ritual was important to Sean and Dez. Practicing routines brought them comfort and relieved the anxiety they often felt growing up as two Black boys in the south. They were born and raised in Anderson, SC, a relatively small town where everybody knew everybody. Dez was 3 years older than Sean, and Dez's friends were a little older than he was. There weren't a lot of other kids Sean's age in their neighborhood, so Sean often tagged along with Dez and his friends until they were too old to hang out with (or were getting into trouble). Dez never had a problem finding trouble to get involved in, especially because their mother was not as present as they wanted her to be.

Dez, unlike his brother who had two children, had no children of his own, but he really enjoyed family, so he visited as often as he could. Though he loved Sean's daughter, he felt particularly close to his brother's son, Kamau. It was obvious to everyone that Kamau took after his uncle as far as his looks, mannerisms, and even his actions. But the influence was mutual. Dez wasn't a college graduate and a family man like his brother, and Kamau inspired him to be a better man. Even though Kamau wasn't Dez's son, he took ownership of him like he was—especially when Sean was unwell. When Kamau was two and his sister was a newborn, Sean was in a car accident that was so bad that the doctors said it should have taken him. Thankfully, he survived, but he was left paralyzed from the waist down. Understandably, he had a difficult time with recovery and adjusting to life without full use of his legs. In fact, there was a 3½-year period during which he slept a lot and was on different medicines to help him cope with the depression he experienced as he mourned the loss of his legs. Dez loved his brother and his family and wanted to ensure that they never experienced the lack that he and his brother experienced when they were young, so he stepped in and took Kamau under his wing. Dez's support really helped Sean get well. Once he recovered from the surgeries and developed healthy strategies to heal from his depression, Sean spent all his time with his children. Because Kamau's mother, Sean's wife Joan, was a middle-school teacher, she spent a lot of time at her school. Immediately after Sean's accident, they became a single-income family, so she worked hard to maintain a comfortable lifestyle for them. Once he returned to work, they agreed that he would work from home so that he could benefit from being able to be a bigger part of Kamau and his sister's life.

Dez had moved to North Carolina for work right after Kamau was born, but he had ritualized coming to visit his Harlem family and stealing his nephew away for the summer—every summer since he was 3 years old. That was his way of sheltering Kamau from some of the stuff his father was going through.

Dez continued to dribble the ball as he walked around the court, "Yup, he needs Big Unc to show him the reason behind some of the things he's doing and teach him to understand life a bit better. Last week, when I spoke to him on the phone, I was telling him that when I was his age, I knew a lot more things than he knows now, things I consider to be common sense, while he knows more about video games and the such than I do." He held the ball and looked at his brother, "He thinks I don't have common sense. I get the feeling his mind is already getting wrapped around the wrong things. I bet his mind is getting wrapped around females and running after females, and while he's with me, I try to focus him more on school and the game." Dez bounced the ball to Sean.

Sean grabbed the ball and held it in his lap. He looked at his brother, "I'd appreciate that, Big Brother." He took a shot. "Yo, Remember, we grew up with RIF: Reading Is Fundamental. Remember that? All those infomercials and shows. It's like they don't have that kind of stuff on TV anymore. I'm looking around, and I'm watching what my kids watch. I'm like, 'Where are all the shows that educate you?' Where are the cartoons that had a moral at the end of the story, where they took time out to actually make sure you understood that yes, this was a cartoon but you got something out of it. I remember watching G.I. Joe and He-Man and She-Ra and all of them. They always had a message at the end. Remember our parents used to tell us that we'd get reinforcement from things that we enjoy? Kids just don't get that anymore."

"I'm all the way there with you, Bro. All the way. They can still watch those shows on YouTube, but it ain't the same. As a matter of fact—" Dez interrupted himself, "Kamau! Come here, Shorty!" Uncle Dez yelled at their first-floor apartment window for his nephew, Kamau, to join the two brothers outside on the basketball court.

"Hey Unc!" Kamau yelled joyfully as he peeped out his bedroom window. "Let me get my kicks." Kamau pulled the tan window shade down, ran to get his red and black Nikes from the living room, and sat down in the kitchen to put them on. He was excited to see his Uncle Dez. Not only did Kamau absolutely adore hanging out with him, but he also loved watching the two brothers interact. He often wondered what it would be like to have a brother. He looked up at his sister's seventh-grade school picture on the refrigerator. Sisters were cool, but he bet having a brother would be even more cool. He ran outside, slamming the steel apartment door behind him. He jogged down the hallway through the building door and right toward his uncle.

Dez gave Kamau a pound,[37] pulled him close for a big hug, then pulled back to look at him. "How are you almost as taller as me?" Dez looked his nephew from head to toe. "You're gonna be taller than your father soon!" The three men laughed. Sean shook his head. He was only 5'7".

Sean took a shot at the basket and laughed, "I see y'all got jokes! But you guys seem to forget which one of us went to college on a basketball scholarship." Nothing but net.

"That's all you, Dad," Kamau smiled at his father. He caught the ball as it swished through the net and palmed it. He thought for a second, then asked, "When you went to college to play ball, did you know you wanted to be a teacher?"

Sean responded, "Nah. Growing up, we were always into sports and other activities. Sports were a big part of my and your uncle's life. We're bigtime competitors; everything we do we try to compete and to win. That's pretty much the way we grew up. Initially, I had no thought of being a teacher. My goal was to be a professional athlete—basketball of course. But … uhm … that didn't work out." Sean shrugged his shoulders. "I mean, I'm like 5'7", so height-wise, it was definitely a long shot. I do know of some dudes on the shorter side who have made it to the NBA." Sean paused, then continued, "I just decided to focus on learning. I remember the light clicked on when I was in fifth or sixth grade; that's when I first started taking academics seriously. I still played middle school and high school sports, and I did well. So good that I got a scholarship to play college ball. They wanted your uncle Dez to play baseball." Sean stole the ball from his son and shot another basket.

Dez chased the rebound and dribbled the ball between his legs. Jump shot. "I can remember as far back as when I was 10 years old; I wanted to be a pediatrician because I wanted to care for kids."

Kamau and Sean laughed, "Wow, YOU? really?" they asked jokingly and in unison.

Dez laughed with them. He continued, "It may seem funny, but I remember watching one of those infomercials on TV. When we were growing up, Ethiopia was a big thing with the starving children and things over there. I remember watching one of those and feeling sad. I wanted to help kids in need." He passed the ball from hand to hand, "I guess that's why I like hanging around here." He threw the ball to Kamau—who laughed as he caught it and stepped out to shoot a three. The ball bounced off the back of the rim, and he ran across the yard to retrieve it.

Sean and Dez looked at each other and shrugged.

Dez watched his nephew attempt another three-pointer and shook his head. Even though their father has been very much present in his life for the last 10 years, Dez was committed to making sure that his niece and nephew would have the best opportunities in life. This basketball game was part of their ritual, and since he didn't see his nephew all the time, he used this time to see where he was mentally and socially. Then, he took it from there. "So how you do in school this year?"

Kamau took a deep breath. He knew this question was coming, and he was dreading it. However, he knew there was no way to avoid it, so he answered honestly, "This year, I was the worst student ever." He dribbled the ball and attempted another three.

The three Miller men briefly laughed at Kamau's candor.

Dez grabbed the ball and passed it to Kamau. "What's up with that?" Dez asked.

Kamau straightened his face and looked up at the basket. "I used to hate school. I hated going to school ... uhmm ... school was just always a struggle for me. I used to not make the A Honor Roll, A/B Honor Roll, none of that back in middle school. But this year ..." Kamau stood on his toes and shot from the free throw line—SWISH, "... I made it: A/B Honor Roll." He held his arm straight up in the air in celebration of the basket he made and his academic success.

"You had me scared, Man! I'm proud of you! That's what's up!" Dez replied clapping for his nephew.

"It was a surprise to me. I really don't know what happened," Kamau shrugged his shoulders and laughed. "It was a struggle in middle school, and so it was a real shock when this year, I made the Honor Roll. I mean ... I've *always* struggled in school. It's never been one easy year where I can say I really liked going to class. You guys know that. But now, some of that has changed."

"What's changed, son?" Sean asked. He was proud of his son, and he thought he knew what was different for Kamau, but he wanted to hear him say it.

Dez jumped in, "Yeah. What motivated you to change how you experienced school?"

Kamau nodded at his dad and looked at his uncle, "It's like … when you experiencing school and doing it on your own and studying on your own and Mom and Dad's not chasing you down for grades and homework and report cards, and you know you gotta get it done. My motivation was to get it done, so I didn't have to come home and hear their mouths complaining about me not doing what I was supposed to be doing in school," Kamau took two steps out of his father's reach and laughed. He continued, "so I think that was the motivation in itself to not have to be nagged about not doing well."

Sean scowled and raised his left fist at Kamau. Dez stepped in between the two of them with his arms stretched as if attempting to break up a fight. Sean laughed and waved his hand at the two of them.

Kamau dribbled the ball through his legs and from left to right. He stopped and turned to his uncle. With his father looking on from his right, Kamau got serious for a second. He said, "Uncle Dez, it was still a struggle, uhmm, but I knew the importance of it. You know my parents were valedictorians in school. They were *studied* students. My dad was, I think uhmm, a high honors graduate from college, and my mom was a A/B student in college, so you know, and they're *teachers*, so you feel me?"

Dez nodded in agreement. He definitely understood how intimidating his brother and sister-in-law's academic prowess could be.

Kamau continued, "The two of them, you feel me, and their drive for success pressured me into being like, okay, I understand why I gotta go to school so …" He shrugged, "I did my best. I decided that if I was to ever fail a class, it wasn't gonna be because I didn't try or didn't do my work; it would be that I simply didn't get it. Being in a new school and all, I guess my drive was just *Okay, I gotta get it this time around. Whatever I missed or didn't do last year, I gotta do different because I gotta face those two.*" Kamau laughed hard. "And being that I'm a peaceful person, I don't like being confronted with conflict. You know, '*Did you do your homework? Let me see*'. So I just felt like I didn't have no choice but to do better."

Sean laughed so hard he had to hold his stomach. "I ain't never heard of a student doing well in school just because he didn't want to hear his parents' mouths, but if you like it, I love it!" He caught his breath and shared, "Thank God you are learning and understanding. The lessons fathers teach are hard; we may not always be right or respond correctly, but I always remind my children that you are blessed because you have a father and a mother who care for you and love you."

Kamau smiled at his father, "I know, Dad."

Sean continued, "Good. School wasn't always easy for me either, but I was taught to understand that it takes hard work to achieve my goals and life desires, much of which was instilled in me by your grandfather."

Kamau nodded, "Ya know, one thing I saw in school this year? A lot of other kids don't have the love they need shown to them from a father. Like, they have mothers trying to pour into them as much as they can, but it seems like mothers can only do so much. Without this, like, 'fatherly love' given to them, they don't have the support and praise they need." Kamau dribbled the ball. "They don't have that father figure to tell them *No, not this way son but that way*. Fathers—you guys—do so much without even knowing it. Some of the kids I met this year go to gangs or spend all their time looking at videos, like, to fill a void—all because they don't have a father in the house … or one close by. I don't want to sound too corny, but I appreciate you guys because of that." Kamau smiled awkwardly at his father and uncle. He was telling the truth, but he truly had no idea he felt this way. He had never said anything like this to either of them, and he hoped that it didn't come back to bite him in the butt.

"Thanks for saying that, Son," Sean said through a big smile.

Dez said, "Maaaaannn, that's what's up! You know, I believe that without fathers, the responsibility falls back on all of us as Black males. We, as males, have the responsibility to tell them *No son, not that way, but this way*. That falls back on us."

Sean asserted, "Sooooo much falls on us. We can't leave these young cats out here haphazardly trying to figure out the definition of a man and how that relates to their own lives. I struggled somewhat with that concept from time to time, and our father was in my life actively 100%. I saw some things growing up, but I'll tell you … I had to do a lot of things on my own. I had to step up to the plate. Most things my dad made us or let us figure out on our own. His thing was to raise us and make sure we had what we needed. He allowed us to make our own decisions, but for the most part, that quest to manhood was our own journey to make."

This conversation had Dez listening closely and reflecting on his own walk. He placed his right hand on the right handle of Sean's chair, leaned on it, and added, "I'll keep it real with you, Nephew. For many years, there was a certain level of confidence I lacked in being a man. I knew how to perform to get attention, but being a man, I didn't know how to be that. I could use my body to get attention from the ladies. I was strong, so I could get respect from other men, but being a man to me meant more than that, but I didn't know how to be a man. I knew how to be a lot of things that made up a man but still didn't really define me as a man. The fact that I could bench 350 didn't define me as man; the fact that I was ranked in the nation in a few sports didn't define me as a man. All the girls I messed with," Dez punched Kamau in his left arm and smiled, "even *that* didn't define me as a man. Even though men do these things, these things alone don't define a man: it's just stuff some men do. But I wrapped myself up in thinking I was a man because of what I did, not from who I was, … until I had to be there for my family." Dez looked down at his brother's legs and rubbed his brother on the head (in the playful way a big brother would mess with a younger brother). "That's when I saw that I didn't know how really to be a man. I had the activities but not the true mindset of a man! So I changed that."

Sean looked up at his brother and grabbed his hand. He squeezed it until Dez let out a shout and laughed. Sean knew what Dez was talking about. After Sean's car accident, Dez showed up for them in a really powerful way. Before then, Dez had been running the streets and chasing women; it used to be hard to track him down. Now, Sean couldn't get rid of him. That accident changed all their lives.

Kamau bounced the ball on his left side. "You was runnin' 'dem skreets, Uncle Dez?" He laughed. He had heard stories of Dez's "wild days," but this was the first time Dez had talked about them in front of Kamau.

"Yo," Dez started, "See, I was a bit more of a wild boy than your dad was. I remember sometimes I wouldn't be home when it got dark, and our dad would come looking for me. He had this car that had a loud muffler on it, and I could hear it blocks away. When I'd hear it, I would run, jump ditches, everything trying to get away, and I would end up beating him home. And ... oh yeah ... there was one *particular* time—I don't ever remember your grandfather whipping your father—but I remember one time he got me. I took the keys to the lawn mower, and *this cat*," Dez pointed to Sean, "and his little friends were like, 'Dez took it! Dez took the keys!' so I went to give the keys back over to your grandfather, and I was trying to ... we had a porch right, ... and instead of walking up the porch to give it to him, I walked to the side of the porch, and I handed the keys to him." Dez and Sean started laughing hard. "That man reached down and grabbed me, yanked me up a few times, and smacked me. I was like, 'Dang man!'" Dez was bent over laughing. "But I'm blessed that I didn't get caught doing *half* of the things I used to do."

Dez and Sean continued to laugh. Sean shook his head and grabbed the basketball from Kamau, who was just holding it because he was enthralled by Uncle Dez's story.

Uncle Dez continued, "And I wasn't half the student your father was. I was good at sports, but I learned differently. I was good at pretending to be engaged in class but really wasn't. I had some really good teachers growing up. But in that small town, those teachers had my uncles, they taught my aunts, they knew the whole family. So they expected me to be like them, but I just learn differently. When they had us doing group work, I wasn't doing the work. I always talked other kids into doing the work and me getting the credit." Dez popped his imaginary collar and winked at his nephew.

Kamau got excited, "You was runnin' the school, too, Unc?!"

"Please don't be like your Uncle," Sean interrupted, shaking his head.

Dez winked at his brother, "Just a lil bit." He held up his right hand, brought his thumb and index finger close together in front of his left eye, and chuckled. He continued, "But not all the time though. I had this one male teacher, Mr. Brown, that was my seventh-grade teacher. He was also my baseball coach. He was the one who could relate to us. He was young, and the stuff we were getting into, he already knew we were doing and would beat us to the punch. He'd let us know, 'Hey, you don't need to be doing that' and helped guide us in the right direction. He was one that I remember just being a male role model. I had a few male teachers, but he's the one that I remember the most. To be honest, the teachers I remember the most are the ones who held me accountable: Mr. Brown was one of the main ones—as far as having an influence on me. But if I knew back then some of the things I know now, then I would have been a much better student. I was just a knucklehead back then."

Sean, seizing the opportunity to tease his brother, said with a grin, "Awww don't feel bad, big brother. You're still a knucklehead."

"Ha Ha Ha," Dez laughed mockingly.

Kamau laughed at his father and uncle. He knew not to get in the middle when they started messing with one another, and he was grateful to have them both in his life in such a big way. He thought about what his uncle had shared about his schooling experience and offered, "I have only had one male teacher, back in the second grade, and he was the only one until … until I got to high school this year. I had a Black male teacher this year in school. That's probably why I liked school again because when I think about it, second grade was my favorite year in school. I still can remember my second-grade teacher's name, but some of my other teachers, I don't even remember their names." Kamau shrugged.

"Well, I'm glad you had a good Black male teacher this year to whip you back into shape! I'm grateful for the help because I was starting to get worried about you," Sean added.

Kamau smiled and nodded at his dad.

Dez responded, "I agree with your father. That's really good." Dez bounced the basketball, looked at the basket and bent his knees, preparing to take a shot, then stopped, "How you doing with the girls, Nephew? They motivating you to do better as well?" Dez shot the ball and made the basket.

Kamau caught the ball as it fell through the hoop and bounced it. He walked toward his uncle and replied, "I haven't really focused on girls or other people in school. The only other person I can say I focused on was my sister. This is our first year in two different schools, so I was just worried about her being okay without me. I just didn't have time to focus on anyone else."

Uncle Dez responded, "I'm glad you're looking out for your sister like that. You know your Aunt Libby was in school at the same time as me. She was liked at school and did well in school. She always succeeded, made the honor roll. Even though she was younger than me, at one point in high school, we were in the same Algebra class. I remember she got an A, and I got a C." Dez shook his head, and Sean laughed.

Sean interrupted, "I remember that!"

Dez shook his head again and laughed, "The teacher sat me down, made my assigned seat next to her, you know. She said 'If you need your sister's help, don't be afraid to ask her—even on a test'. This teacher gave me permission to cheat on a test! I never did 'cause I didn't want Libby telling our father."

"That's crazy," Kamau exclaimed. "She gave you permission to cheat like that? And you didn't?!" He laughed. "But I feel you. It always seems like the boys get in trouble more than girls. Uhm ... it just seemed that there was always a lot more attention on boys than other groups in that class. And I feel that, in high school, I feel that there are certain ... uh ... I guess careers that the girls are kinda pushed towards, and there are certain careers that we are pushed towards. That's different from middle school, and I definitely feel the difference."

"Which careers were you guys encouraged to pursue?" Sean asked his son. He was not aware that this was happening at Kamau's school.

Kamau replied, "I feel that girls, and specifically Black girls are pushed more to education honestly. And the Black males, we are pushed to more so things to do with engineering, uhm ... and architecture and that sort of thing."

"Hmmm. That's interesting, Son. I'm not feeling that ... at all. I'm going to talk with your mother about this. I wonder if she's aware." Sean leaned back in his chair, crossed his arms, and touched his chin with his left hand.

"So last summer, you was all about HipHop—trying to be a gangster rapper. You thinking about engineering or architecture now ... or still tryna be Mr. Gangsta HipHop?"

Kamau smiled at his uncle. Uncle Dez had been teasing Kamau for wanting to be a rapper for several years now, and though he didn't necessarily want to be a rapper anymore, he wasn't sure what he wanted to be when he grew up. He shared, "Nah Unc, I'm not tryna be a rapper anymore, but I love HipHop. It's my life, how I dress, and act. But it has never made me want to be a gangster to do anything illegal or to be disrespectful to my elders. I think it's cool, but I know the difference between a positive message and a bad one."

Dez raised his right eyebrow, "Oh yeah. Who you listening to?"

Kamau continued, "My favorites are Heavy D & Da Boyz, Queen Latifah, A Tribe Called Quest, Big Daddy Kane, and Kool Moe Dee. They know how to have fun and make me think about life. It's like I feel their lyrics deep in my soul. They are great lyricists *and* artists. I mean, they've all had their beefs, but they settle it on the track. They rap about having better lives, education, history, and overall consciousness. Most of them are educated and never gotten into any trouble with the law. They make HipHop the art form that it is today because what they say has substance. Ya know, I just would like to live in a world that isn't filled with drama and worries that way people could concentrate on becoming that person who could positively contribute to our society."

"I love to hear that, Son," Sean rolled over to Kamau and pat him on the back. "You're getting less like your uncle and more like your good ole-dad every day!" Sean winked at Dez who had waved his hand at Sean.

Kamau laughed at his uncle and looked at his dad. His face turned serious, "For real though, you really inspire me, Dad. Like, after your accident, you went back to college and got your Master's degree at an older age. And then, uhm ... became a college professor. And so ... uhm ... that kind of, you know, sparked my interest in school. You and Mom have always pushed education at home. You know, you being a professor, and, you know, just all through my life, you know, just made sure I always knew how important education is. That kind of helped me be on track."

"Wow Son. I didn't know you were watching like that!," Sean reached up and hugged his son, "I'll tell you the truth. I was not really excited about going back to school, *especially* after my accident, but my father always said, 'you may not be the best'," Dez joined in and the brothers continued in unison, "*but at least you have to try.*" Sean and Dez laughed.

Sean continued, "You know, because sometimes you get to those points where you don't want to do nothing, and you might have those teachers who encourage you to always do your best. But you know your family—we are the type to try, we don't just quit, I was never just taught to quit and roll over and give up, so I had to get up. My parents never gave up on me, and if I am going to be the same way, then I can't give up on myself. And I'll never give up on you or your sister. You, your sister, your mother—you guys are my life. You understand? Okay, Son?"

"Yes, Dad. I do." Kamau hugged his father again.

Dez threw his hands in the air and cried aloud in a joking manner, "Awwww I love you guys, too! Gimme a hug!"

The three Miller men laughed at Dez and hugged one another tight.

As an adult, Kamau often thought about the moments he spent on the basketball court with his father and uncle. Those were such good times. His folks weren't perfect, but even as a teenager, Kamau knew that he gotten his nurturing nature from his father always being there for him and with him all the time. He also knew how valuable his Uncle Dez's presence was in his life. And as he grew and matured into a man, he did what he was always around and was used to seeing and doing—respecting ritual, giving credit where credit is due, and changing for the better.

CHAPTER 4
I Can't Hug the Kids[38]

Kamau Miller loved being back home. He loved it because he was a star in his hood. His boys were there. His family was there. And he loved how the old heads treated him because of how he treated them: with mutual respect and love. Don't get me wrong; he loved the Hill, where he has lived for the past 5 years and teaches third grade at Derrick Bell Elementary School. He loves teaching there, and he loves his students: he calls them his "Little homies." But New York City was HOME. It was where he could spread his wings and be himself. It's where his family and his oldest friends were. Most importantly, it's where Rucker Park was! Yep, The Rucker was where legends were made and legends-in-the-making played. Rucker Park is a historic and world-renowned basketball court in Harlem, and it was only a few blocks from Kamau's sister's apartment (where he stayed whenever he was in town). And Kamau loved catching up with his boys at the Rucker. They would joke one another and share their latest adventures, while playing ball or sitting and watching a game, while waiting to get next.

The three friends could hear the deejay playing "Star in Da Hood" from three blocks away, and Black Rob[39] led the way as the three friends walked to the park. The park was not as full as it normally was, so Kamau sat next to his longtime friends, Adam and Terence, on the first row of the bleachers. Eric, a young brother Kamau had never met before, walked up to them and asked, "Yo, mind if I run with you guys?"

Kamau replied, "Sure, young cat. You make four. What's your name? I'm Kamau." Kamau looked at his friends and nodded. "These my boys, Adam and Terence."

Adam and Terence stood up and gave Eric a pound and said, "Sup man?"

Eric was younger than Kamau and his friends. Eric was 17 years old and a senior at A. Phillip Randolph Campus High School[40] in Harlem. However, it did not matter to him that he was several years younger than his new teammates because Eric loved to play ball, and that's why he liked to hang at the Rucker. Eric responded, "Nice to meet you guys," then he tossed his basketball back and forth in his hands, looking back and forth between the guys and the court, "You bruhs play here on the reg?"[41]

"Here and there," Terence said, "especially when my man is in town."

Eric looked at Kamau, and Kamau added, "Yeah. I'm from Frederick Douglass Projects, but I live out in the Hill now—That's the Hill District in Pittsburgh. I teach out there."

"The Hill?" Eric nodded, "I got family out there. I used to go out there all the time when I was little. It's tough out there. How you like it?" He sat down next to Kamau.

"You're right; it's tough, but I do my best to take care of my lil homies." Kamau smiled.

"Your lil homies?" Eric laughed.

Laughing, Adam pinched the shoulder of Kamau's shirt and said, "Yeah. He's talking about his students. They gave him this cute lil shirt." Kamau was wearing a yellow tee shirt with "Derrick Bell Elementary" printed in large font on the front of the shirt. The 26 third graders in Kamau Miller's class had signed their names in varying forms of script, filling in much of the blank yellow space on the front and back of the shirt. Terence started laughing with Adam.

"Stop hatin'!" Kamau laughed. "My kids love me, and I love them."

Eric stopped laughing and focused his gaze on the court but was intrigued by Kamau's last statement, "What made a brother from Frederick Douglass become a teacher?"

Kamau explained, "My moms was a teacher, and when I was younger, whenever I was out of school, I would spend a lot of time tutoring and volunteering in her classroom, ya know, to stay out of trouble myself. This kinda built a strong passion to work with children; it also brought to my attention that a lot of young men don't have positive role models to choose from, so I decided that I would become one. But you know what? I fought it at first. I tried going to school to study business, but it didn't stick. Ya feel me? Some people spend their whole lives searching for that thing that makes sense … that thing that makes their heart beat. *But I knew right off the bat this was the right thing for me.*"

"Hmm" Eric began. "Word. So you went to school for that?" Eric handed Kamau the basketball as if he were handing him a talking stick.

Kamau dribbled the ball between his feet and thought for a second. He loved talking about what he did—his job and his kids, but he knew that he could get passionate about the topic and didn't want to get clowned by this new cat. He palmed the ball in both hands, shrugged his shoulders, then went for it: "Yeah. I went to Hunter College, and when I did my student teaching, *I fell in love with the little kids* …. I did 4th grade for my student teaching, and I loved it. Every day of it was great—even the bad days I miss, you know? And those kids … it's different in the City than in Pittsburgh, but near Hunter, with those kids, it was a lot of love. Like they see me in the morning, their faces light up, come give me a hug, and made me feel good. I'd hug them back, and we'd have a good day. Now, in Pittsburgh, the kids are a little different—the culture's different. I can't hug the kids just because it would be taken the wrong way."

Adam shook his head. "It always bugs me out when you talk like that about your students. You my man and all, but you gotta be careful when you talk about how much you love your kids and be hugging on them and stuff like that."

Terence jumped in: "But why? Now you've known this man since y'all was in the 8th grade. You know he ain't no pedophile, and yo' mama knows he ain't gay!"

Adam pushed Terence, and the four guys all laughed.

Adam asserted, "Of course I know my bruh ain't gay or no pedophile, but everybody else don't know that, and unfortunately, that's what some people think about Black men who teach little kids."

"Yeah, I know what they think," Kamau started, "and that's probably one of the hardest parts of my job—not the ever-changing curriculum, not the important responsibility that comes with mentoring children, not the low pay—but dealing with the stereotypes from people who believe that I'm doing white women's work. They're waiting for white women to come in and save the day—be the Great White Hope, like in *Freedom Writers* or *Dangerous Minds*. It definitely sucks that more males of color aren't elementary teachers because these kids need it. They need to see figures like me and other brothers who are passionate about learning, passionate about education, and are going to be there to help them to be the best that they can be. But instead, we gotta watch how we talk and every little thing we do instead of focusing on showing these children, especially Black boys, the door of opportunity. I mean, it's always shut in front of them." Kamau tossed the ball between his hands and stared into space. His mind was back in the Hill.

He continued, "One particular Black boy, when I first started at my school—I was tutoring in the 3rd grade and teaching the 4th …. The 3rd grade teacher had nothing good to say about him—nothing good at all. I would just sit there like, 'What you mean you don't have nothing good to say about this kid? This boy was bright. You know?' And it's like, looking at it from her perspective, she said that he was the worst of the worst. I got the same boy in my class that next year. He scored at the Proficient level on the PSSA[42] in language arts and math, the first time around. I was like, he was never (laughs)—I mean from what I saw that year—he was never 'the worst', you know what I'm saying? But from her perspective, that's what he was. And that's how she treated him, to the point where he couldn't succeed, but with the right opportunity, he succeeded."

Kamau dribbled the ball with one hand. He passed the ball to Terence just as the deejay mixed in LL Cool J's "I Need Love."[43] Terence laughed and rapped along as the song played.

"Maaaaaaaaaaaan! LL changed the game when he dropped this one! Nobody was talking about love and stuff like that before L. He made it okay for brothers to be all vulnerable and stuff." Adam laughed at himself, "But you don't know nothing about that, Youngin'. You young cats are too hard for that, right?" Adam teased Eric.

Eric laughed with Adam, shook his head, and said, "Nah. We not all like that." Then, he looked back at Kamau, who had truly piqued his interest. "So you like helping the kids?"

Kamau smiled and replied, "Oh man. I love it, and *I need love* in my life. As soon as I started, my mentoring background and tutoring background kicked in, and I was a natural. From day one, when I hit the ground running, I've been educating kids, pushing kids ever since. Real talk: teaching isn't just being in the classroom; it's impacting the lives of people who will impact the future. I mean, when you teach, you're investing in a kid's life—not just book lessons. I take my job very seriously because when I'm in front of a kid, I'm, literally, molding him. I am chipping away at that kid, and that can mean life or death for a young Black male, you feel me? So I take great honor in having the opportunity to teach kids that are not my own because I know that I'm going to go in there and treat them like my own."

"You talk a lot about all the good stuff—how much you love your job and the kids, but it can't be all that hot, right? I'm saying … what do you hate about it?"

Kamau stood up, facing the court, and stretched his arms above his head, sighed, and put his hands on hips. Then, he turned to Eric with a serious, almost sad, look on his face and responded, "When I first came to the Hill, the school principal told me that I must …" Kamau changed his voice to mock his principal's tone, "*refrain from showing the children any hands-on affection.*" He finished, "She said that only a high five or fist bump were appropriate forms of touch for me. When I met the district superintendent, a Brother, he told me that as a Black man, I needed to be extra careful and that I needed to make sure I didn't touch the kids because it would be misconstrued. In a meeting, my grade chair told me that I better not ever try to hug or touch the children in any way. What I'm saying is where I teach, I am reminded every day that because I am a Black man, I can't show any affection to my students, especially the female students, because it *can and will* be seen as something more. When I was working downtown, the parents encouraged hugs and affection, you know? They were happy to know that their kids came to a teacher that gave them love and was able to give them a hug and everything and calm them down. But in the Hill, that kind of affection ain't welcome from a Black man. It's just a fist-bump or a high five: that's it. I mean … I'm a teacher. I'm there to love and nurture these children, so the whole not touching the kids sucks, but I don't have a choice really. I've kinda gotten used to it now. It is not something I like, but I can deal with it. I don't like paying taxes either, but I have to deal with that." Kamau shrugged his shoulders and looked back at the guys playing ball on the court.

Terence tossed the ball to Eric and added, "I've visited this brother at work with his kids." Kamau nodded his head. Terence continued, "And I realized that you have got to be cut out for teaching. You've really got to have a nurturing nature about you, a nurturing spirit. You just can't work with kids and not have that. I saw that. I don't know if all males have that: White or Black."

Kamau asserted, "Not all PEOPLE have that: male or female. Sometimes, you just want to grab up these kids and hug 'em 'cause you know they don't get it anywhere else. But this Black man doesn't because he can't. I can't hug the kids." Kamau sat back down on the bleachers. "But to replace the hug, I high-five everybody I see. I make it a point, sometimes, to go across the cafeteria, or across the classroom, or if I'm walking down the hallway, I see a kid, and he's not looking too happy, then, I stop what I'm doing, and I make it a point to go all the way down the hallway to give him a high-five. And believe it or not, that puts smiles on their faces. Even that kind of affection, that passion, can brighten up a day, just by letting them know that somebody was thinking about them for that moment or that time. So sometimes I feel like my role on some days is just to put a smile on someone's face."

"Passion, huh?" Eric raised an eyebrow as he turned to look at Kamau.

"Yeah. I'm talking about passion." Kamau replied unapologetically.

"You know," Eric started, "I think I know what you're talking about. I had a Black male teacher when I was in the fifth grade, Mr. Lucas. He was around ALL THE TIME. When I was a kid, we just thought he LIVED at the school! Ha! It's like he was the first one at the school and the last to leave. He even came out to support me and other students at our games and stuff on the weekends; he would call our parents to let them know how we were doing—good and bad. He just did all sorts of activities for the school but also in the community. For real, I didn't appreciate it then, but when I think back on it, I realize that he was an African American male that was serious about taking care of our community. He wasn't just a teacher; he was a community leader. I would see him everywhere. It's like he was trying to change the parents, the students, the school, city, state, everything! Is that the passion thing you're talking about?"

Kamau smiled and nodded.

Eric palmed the ball between both hands. "I respected that so much. Mr. Lucas was the man!"

"Yeah man," Kamau asserted, "I don't mean to sound corny, but—"

Adam interrupted, "Oh NOW he trying NOT to sound corny?" He and Terence cracked up.

Kamau laughed under his breath. His homeboys were the only people on this earth who he didn't mind teasing him when it came to his passion for teaching. He just shook his head and continued, "children are not only the future, they are today. The way that we teach them, mold them, commit to them, mentor them, raise them: that is such a vital and important responsibility. I take it on wholeheartedly. It takes a very pure passion to become and remain an elementary school teacher."

"Come on Mr. Elementary School Teacher of Year, Youngin', and KnuckleHead," Terence addressed the three guys sitting with him on the bench as he stood up, "We're up."

The four gentlemen took the court. They played ball. The three friends played rough. In classic "old dude" style, Terence and Adam grabbed the back of Eric's shirt every time he tried to take a jump shot. They laughed as Eric made jokes about how he felt the "old dudes" couldn't keep up with him, and Adam joked Eric for not being able to "see" him past the breastmilk on his breath.

After their game was over, Kamau gave Eric his number and told him to hit him up the next time he was in Pittsburgh or if he wanted someone to talk to about college. The guys exchanged dap[44] and went their separate ways: Adam, Terence, and Kamau back to Frederick Douglass, and Eric crossed the street and entered his apartment building.

As he waited for the elevator, Eric hummed the rhythm to "Star in Da Hood." The elevator arrived, and as Eric attempted to open the door, Trent pulled the door closed and said, "Yo, take the stairs." The building elevator was often used for illegal business transactions, and Eric understood Trent's command to mean that either drug dealing or pimping was happening on the elevator, so he heeded the warning and took the stairs. Thanksgiving changed nothing. Trent was a well-known drug dealer who Eric did not want to cross because he knew that would mean some form of retaliation. Eric did not need nor want that. Besides, this was nothing new for him, and he was feeling energized after the time he spent with Kamau, Adam, and Terence anyway.

When he left his 10th-floor apartment earlier that afternoon, he had no idea he would meet such cool "old dudes." As he returned to his apartment, he was thoughtful. He walked over to the kitchen table and raised his right eyebrow at the half-eaten sweet potato pie his mother had left for him. He smiled and yelled, "Thanks Ma!" to his mother, who he knew was in her bedroom resting.

"You're welcome, Baby!" Eric's mother responded.

Eric shoveled a fork full of pie into his mouth, put the fork down in the pie tin, and then picked up the pile of college applications. He looked at the one on the top, picked up a pencil off the table, found the "Major" section, and erased the checkmark he had placed in the "Undecided" box. He sat down in the chair, placed the applications down in front of him, and looked out the window overlooking Rucker Park. After a few minutes, he looked down at the application, and then checked the box next to "Elementary Education."

CHAPTER 5
You Don't Have to Wonder What My Motives Are

Our fathers and mothers came here, lived, loved, struggled and built here. At this place, their love and labor rose like the sun and gave strength and meaning to the day. For them, then, who gave so much we give in return. On this same soil we will sow our seeds, and liberation and a higher level of human life.[45]

"Ase!" Kamau shouted along with the crowd assembled at the Nafasi on Centre in Pittsburgh.[46] He was attending a pre-Kwanzaa celebration with Diane, the woman he's been dating since April. He looked at Diane. Her head was bowed; her eyes were closed; her arms were bent, elbows close to her sides, and her hands extended in front of her—facing upward. In his eyes, and in his heart, she was stunning. He was grateful to meet a woman as culturally steeped as he was. This was their first Kwanzaa season together, and she had expressed sincere excitement when he asked her to attend the Hill CDC's pre-Kwanzaa celebration at Nafasi then go to the Dazzling Nights[47] walk-through holiday experience at the Pittsburgh Botanic Garden.

"Ase!" The crowd resounded as the speaker continued to recite the *Tamshi la Tambiko* (Kwanzaa libation prayer) at the opening of the pre-Kwanzaa celebration. Kamau was torn between focusing on the empowering libation statement and staring at Diane. She wore African and Afrocentric clothing all the time, and today she was wearing a colorful, fitted, two-piece fishtail African skirt set. Yellow was the main color, but it had patterns of red, blue, and green throughout both pieces. And in true Diane fashion—her own unique style—she was wearing a red head wrap which held up her waist-length auburn locs and red high-heeled Timbs. She was stunning.

"Ase! Ase! Ase-ooooo!" The crowd chanted along with the speaker as they completed the libation statement. Everyone sat down, and as his dad had taught him, he looked at Diane and waited for her to sit before taking his seat next to her. Mutually smitten, they smiled at one another. She took his hand and held it between both of hers on her left leg. She loved that he was such a gentleman.

As the pre-Kwanzaa celebration went on, Kamau thought about his mother. He was so appreciative to have a mom who was such a strong, STRONG, African American woman who believed in empowering her children and her family to know that they are people from a strong bloodline and who are very, very integral to this country. He always reflected on that idea during Kwanzaa. Diane reminded him of his mother. She had that same passion for culture and family.

As they enjoyed the program, he also remembered some of the teachers he's had who made him think about what it means to be an African and American, what it means to identify as an African *and* American in this country? He recalled how they stressed the importance of understanding Black history, the context—bigger than MLK and Rosa Parks, but going all the way back to Timbuktu, Nubia, and Kush—and understanding the impact that his Blackness had on the world. He was grateful that he had teachers who did that, teachers who gave him opportunities to grow as a leader, facilitating opportunities and pushing him to do things that were outside of his comfort level but guiding him along the way while saying, "It's okay. We got you. All you gotta do is just step out there. We have you."

"That was incredible. So powerful and inspiring!" Diane said to Kamau as the crowd loudly held their last Harambee![48]

"It really was. I'm glad you came with me," Kamau responded, "You ready to see the lights?"

Diane looked around the room. There were a few vendors she wanted to check out before they left. "Just let me spend a few more of these Black dollars with these Black vendors, then I'll be good to go. Okay?" She smiled at Kamau.

"Of course, Babe," he replied. He loved that Diane was adamant about supporting Black-owned businesses, and today was no different. He looked forward to the African Marketplace that was typically part of public Kwanzaa celebrations. The Marketplace at this celebration was bustling. There were more than a dozen or so vendors spread around the perimeter of the room. They each adorned their six foot tables differently—their wares strewn about in creative, inviting ways that highlighted their key products.

Kamau accompanied Diane as they walked around the colorful, large, bright room. She was lively and friendly. She talked to different merchants, asking lots of questions about their goods, and asking his opinion on different items. They stopped at one table where the elder Black woman was selling replicas of lighthouses.

Kamau laughed, "Oh wow! Diane, look at this." He picked up a clay lighthouse that was painted in shiny shades of beige, blue, and green and showed it to Diane. "One time when I was little, we had to make a replica of a state. I had North Carolina, and it had to like, show the regions and have texture and all these things. So … I didn't have a lot to use, so my mom and I used my sister's hair beads." They laughed; then, he continued, "My mother, she can draw, like, she can draw so well, and she drew the replica of North Carolina. Then, we glued the beads on, and so the red ones were the coastal plains, the white ones were the Piedmont, and then the green—no they were red, white, and blue. The blue was the mountains. It might've been the first time I did a color scheme, and then, we also had to do a lighthouse replica—of one of the lighthouses in the state. And, if you could've seen what some of the kids turned in." They laughed.

Diane giggled, "Stop talking about your friends!"

"Nah," Kamau laughed, "I'm sayin' like some of their parents went all out, and they made them out of wood and bricks, and like it was a real working lighthouse, just small. And mine," He shook his head with a smile, "mine was a piece of posterboard rolled up like a cone …" he made a rolling motion with his hands, "and painted and drawn on. We took some more construction paper, cut out the pieces that were supposed to be lifted out, like the uhm, what's it called? The part you step on out the window?"

"The balcony?" Diane asked holding back a laugh.

"Yeah! The balcony! It was made out of construction paper, and we glued it on. It had a base, and we drew on the water and everything, so it would look like a river around the lighthouse. I got an A on both projects—off effort and originality." Kamau finished feeling proud of himself as he continued to admire the elder's high-quality handcrafted lighthouses.

Deciding to bypass the lighthouses, Diane began admiring a Bronx tee-shirt on the table next to the lighthouse table. She looked back at Kamau and stated, "Money isn't everything." The couple laughed and agreed.

The next table was manned by a light-skinned brother named Shawn, along with his son, Anwar, and two daughters, Ausaria and Alannah. Anwar greeted Diane and Kamau, "*Habari Gani?*" Diane smiled at the young man and responded accordingly, "*Umoja!*[49] I love your shirts! Really creative!"

Kamau and Diane perused the tee shirts. There were shirts designed with symbols from each of the five boroughs. Diane, who was from the Bronx, was particularly pleased to see a vendor selling NYC gear. Shawn shared that he was originally from Brooklyn and had been teaching his children how to create and sell art. Upon finding out Diane was from the Bronx, he directed her attention to his HipHop collection. She called Kamau's attention to a pile of shirts decorated with different HipHop artists.

"Ooooh! Who are your favorite HipHop artists?" She asked Kamau.

Kamau, who had been talking to the youngest daughter, Alannah, about the paintings on the table that she had made, replied, "My favorite of all time is BIG. I can't say anything bad about the guy. Every song was great. Jay, of course, and then 50, Jeezy, and I like J Cole, too." He looked through the tee shirts. Shawn had created shirts featuring each of Kamau's favorites. He looked at Shawn and said, "I see you have all the greats here." Then, he looked over to Diane, who was on his left and asked, "What about you?"

Diane commented, "BIG is my all-time favorite, but 50 is my—that's who I listen to the most. I love all 50's music. He's my favorite rapper right now. I remember the first mixtape of his I heard was—it came on with—it was a little freestyle, and when he ended, he was talking like, *The effin' price went up 10 grand this effin' week*"[50] She chuckled.

Unable to help himself, Anwar jumped in, "I've heard that mixtape! It just sounded so cool." He laughed. "I didn't ever sell drugs or anything like that, but it sounded so cool the way he said on that track, *We can't get money selling weed? (We gon' sell coke)*[51]! I've listened to the whole mixtape repeatedly, and he was killing it. My older cousin, James, he was the one who found it for to me. And it's ironic that you mentioned it because he just called me. He works oversees on a contract with the military in Iraq, and right now, he's got a government job. He's in DC. He called me on Tuesday night and was playing that exact line on the phone—just to let me hear it because he's the one who put me on to it. So ever since I've been a big 50 Cent fan, too."

Diane smiled at Anwar, "Ahhight young blood! You talked about 50, and you didn't even mention Power! How old are you? Do you remember *How to Rob*[52]?"

"I'm 23, but yup, that was on the *In Too Deep* soundtrack. I heard he made a lot of people mad with that one," Anwar laughed. "But I'm not gonna lie. I used to have that same attitude. I didn't care about what nobody said or how they acted. That's another thing that made me like him a lot. I could fight. I never lost a fight after age 11."

Shawn shook his head at his son's confession and joined the conversation, "Yeah, my kids inherited their love for HipHop from me." He looked at his three children with pride and continued, "One of my favorites is Dear Mama by Tupac. I mean who doesn't love their mama and her being the matriarch and the superwoman of the world? Especially Black mothers! You know, they are the epitome of strength, pride, and everything, anything that's spiritual, they represent. And to know that he wrote a song to his mom saying, *Well you know I wasn't the best man I could be, but I definitely am trying. I love you. Thank you for embracing me for who I am even the times when I was a knucklehead.*" Shawn lightly tapped his son in the chest. Anwar faked like he was hurt from the jab and held his chest. The father and son laughed. "Yes, yes. I think one of my favorite lines from that song ... so he's honest about who he is—*I was a knucklehead*—but he even says, *Even though you were a crack fiend, Mama, you always were a Black Queen Mama*,[53] It's such a powerful idea there, ... I know ... I'm not perfect, and you're not perfect, but I still love you. That transcends all of that. Oh, and even though it's not a HipHop song, he wrote a poetry book called *A Rose Grows From Concrete*. It's really good."

"Oh for sure," Kamau started, "I've read his poetry book. Great stuff there! That boy was talented!"

Diane picked up a KRS-One shirt and held it up to Kamau's chest. She looked over at the girls and asked, "What about you two young ladies? Y'all like HipHop like your father and brother?"

The oldest daughter, Ausaria, pleased to be invited into the conversation, happily jumped in, "Ooh, I love Tupac. I love Common. Right now I'm listening to Canton Jones because he's a gospel rapper, so I like him. I love Queen Latifah. I think she's positive. I love Floetry. I know they're more R&B/Soul, but they have a nice flow. I still like them, so I put them in the HipHop realm. I hated when they broke up."

The youngest daughter, Alannah, chimed in, "Ooooh. Nas and Lauryn Hill!" She started singing and snapping her fingers, "I love it love it babaaaaayyy," Alannah and Ausaria laughed. Alannah continued, "That's one of my favorite songs."

Kamau was pleased by this interaction and was glad Diane wanted to take some time to interact with some of the cool folk present before leaving the pre-Kwanzaa celebration. This was definitely the place to be at this moment: Black culture, Black entrepreneurism, Black music, Black love, Black family—just pure, beautiful Blackness all around him. He smiled, "That's wassup! You guys are hyped about *If I Ruled the World*, and that song is a bit before your time. Why do you like that song so much?"

Alannah smiled a big smile. She was so happy that someone actually wanted to talk to her about something other than what's on the table. She responded, "Because it allows you to believe that anything is possible, the impossible is possible. Uhm ... that you are not governed by a certain lifestyle, socio-economic status, certain neighborhood—just the premise that you can be anything you want to be. And I just love it. I love just that even Nas and Lauryn Hill are still so relevant, even though that song is probably almost 20 years old—*older than me …* but not by too much. I'm 16. It's just still relevant. Uhm … and when I play it for my friends, even they are like 'Oh yeah!'" She clapped her hands and danced behind their vendor's table. "I love it love it babaaaaayyy." The five of them laughed.

Kamau reached over to the right of the table and picked up a poster with A Tribe Called Quest on it. "This is the greatest, greatest, greatest, greatest rap group of all time right here." He showed the poster to Diane. "That's hands down. That's my favorite group right there. I can take the whole Midnight Marauders album and play the whole thing all the time."

Diane smiled and nodded her head, "For sure! The Tribe is everything!" Looking from Kamau to Shawn and back to Kamau, she asked, "You guys remember when Video Music Box was out?"

The two men nodded and said, "Sure do" almost in unison.

"When that came out, that revolutionized the video world. We would sit there after school and on Saturday afternoons and watch video after video," Diane responded. She picked up a black tee shirt with a white shadowed image of Kid'n'Play on it. "Kid'n'Play! That's another group that I really like. I mean … The Jungle Brothers, De La Soul, definitely all the conscious rap groups like Public Enemy … I just feel their influence, you know?"

"Okay, if I go all the way back to when I was a kid," Kamau inserted, "I was born after Grandmaster Flash and Kurtis Blow, and I was influenced by them. I really like Kool Moe Dee, Slick Rick, and Doug E. Fresh. I definitely also like Heavy D & the Boyz and Queen Latifah, like the young princess here." Kamau pointed his hand at Ausaria.

She smiled and leaned her head toward her right shoulder as if to say *Thank you.*

Kamau smiled at the family. Their artwork was impressive, and he and Diane had found several pieces they really liked. Diane had separated out a black tee shirt with a black and white picture of KRS-One on the cover of his *By All Means Necessary* album, a tan hoodie with a crown-wearing

Queen Latifah looking up to the sky, and the poster of the mural on Linden Boulevard in Queens of A Tribe Called Quest's *Midnight Marauders* album cover. Kamau paid for the three items, and he and Diane said their goodbyes to Shawn and his family.

As they walked away from the table, Diane looked at Kamau and said, "*They* were cool! I want to have children like that some day."

Kamau smiled, "Yeah. They were really cool. I love how knowledgeable they were about HipHop, even the girls."

Diane stopped in her tracks, "Excuse me. What you mean by that?" She turned and faced Kamau in the middle of the large room, people walking and talking and shopping, all around them.

Kamau grabbed Diane by the hands and laughed, "My bad! I'm not saying that girls don't know HipHop. I was just pointing out that the young princesses were super HipHop aware. That's all." He smiled, hoping his response would soothe Diane.

Diane raised her right eyebrow and closed her left eye, "Hmm ... okay. Let's go look at some lights." She headed toward the room's exit. The door was decorated with yellow, orange, blue, and red kente cloth—a different design but similar colors to her outfit. She asked Kamau to take her picture in the doorway and then they took a selfie together before they left the event.

Kamau opened the car door for Diane and asked, "Did you enjoy that?"

"Thank you," she smiled as she got into the passenger's seat of his car. She continued, "Oh, most certainly. I enjoyed the entire experience— especially that family selling the shirts!"

"Word," Kamau agreed. He closed her door, opened the trunk, and placed the bags with the items they purchased inside. Then, he walked around to the driver's side and got in. He started the car. Though he's lived in Pittsburgh for about 5 years now, he had never been to see the Dazzling Nights exhibit, and he was as excited as little Kamau would've been.

Diane, still thinking about Kamau's *even the girls* statement at Nafasi on Centre, asked, "So ... Kamau, you've been teaching in the school system for a while now, do you feel like girls and boys are seen and/or treated equitably in schools?"

Kamau took a deep breath. Diane was a master's student in the Human Servies program at Lincoln University and has been working as a mental health advocate for the past few years. She was a deep thinker—he loved that about her, as well as her compassion for humanity and passion for helping others—so he knew his statement would not be forgotten so easily. He laughed to himself, but he was confident that Diane knew he wasn't a raving sexist. He thought about his teaching experience, took another deep breath, and responded, "I think Black girls get more attention for some of the wrong things or just different than guys. Guys are seen as more easy-going, more …" Kamau paused, then decided to finish his thought, "sometimes easier to work with, so I think the expectation or the, uhm, stereotype of Black girls is probably that they are difficult to work with, but …" He paused again briefly, kept his face looking forward, and looked at Diane from the side. She had turned to face him and was listening intently.

He continued, "When I was a student, I felt like the girls tried harder to please, trying harder to please their teachers, probably that made it a little easier. Whereas the guys at a younger age are more influenced by their classmates and people in the neighborhood or things of that matter. But girls seem to be a little more independent—meaning if they were bad, they were going to be bad regardless. And if they were good students, they wanted to prove to everybody who was looking or listening that they were a good student. I mean, there's lots of little differences. Girls were always treated a little softer, a little sweeter because they're girls, and they're looked at as such." Kamau shrugged, "When I was young, I've seen situations where the Black girls got away with everything. The teachers were just more lenient towards the girls when they misbehaved, so *a lot* has changed over the years."

"You're right about that! A lot *has* changed," Diane stated. She was shocked but not really surprised by her date's response. They had been dating exclusively for about 5 months now, and she couldn't believe that they'd never had this conversation. She had more questions for Kamau, "So … do you see a difference within the school system with how white and Black teachers treat children?"

Another thing Kamau enjoyed about Diane was that she always engaged him in deep, rich conversations. He relaxed as he realized that he wasn't in any trouble with her for his comment earlier; she was genuinely curious. He shared, "Diane, so many times I've come across teachers who weren't effective in their own practice, their own pedagogy, their own beliefs, thinking statements, beliefs around children of color. When I was growing up, I've had teachers who doubted who I was, tried to make me second guess my own identity as being a Black male."

"Oh, I bet your mother got them straight!" Diane laughed. "I've never met Ms. Joan, but how you describe her, I'm sure she was having none of that." Diane sat back in the passenger's seat.

Kamau nodded and added, "Oh yeah, you know it, but I've had some jacked up experiences, too. For example, Mr. Samuel was my seventh grade math teacher. I think he was, uh, … a younger teacher coming in … uhm … I wanna say he was Irish if I'm not mistaken, and he was trying to find a way to reach us as students, and because I *seemingly* was a little bit more outspoken."

Diane gasped, "You? Outspoken?" She covered her mouth as if in shock and laughed.

Kamau laughed with her. "Oh hush. Let me tell you: sometimes he would take my outspokenness as being a negative: that I was trying to challenge him personally—when instructionally, I was hungry, and I wanted to understand, and so when people … when we as students were confused with something, he took it as if it was an assault on him as a person. He didn't understand that I was always used to being able to ask questions so that I could understand. He felt I was aggressive, was being smart-alecky, that I didn't want to do the work, and it really, really created a dysfunction. I started to have a hate for mathematics—something that I had loved for so long. I started to encounter teachers who weren't effective at what they were doing. They couldn't reach and teach me, so I developed a uhm … I don't want to say it's a phobia, but it was a block that I could not move past … these lessons in mathematics, and I was always doing well. Actually, it impacted and affected me in such a way that it still has some underlying, lingering effects because when I teach my students now, I'm always second guessing myself to see whether or not I'm really … presenting the information and concepts and conceptual thinking in a way that they reach it and understand it. Ya know?"

"Wow, Kamau. I had no idea you had teachers like that," Diane looked at Kamau and looked out the window. She thought about the people she's worked with over the years and the stories they have told about how their schooling experiences have negatively impacted them. She had never known anyone personally with such a story. "I'm glad you were able to persevere, ya know. Succeed despite those challenges."

"Ya know, my dad taught me: *Seek to understand so that you may thrive and grow*. But because of my experiences with that white teacher, I was kicked out of his class. Before then, I had always been on an honors track, and this was an honors class, so I was put in a special ed classroom that same year." Kamau looked down at the GPS on his phone and made a left turn.

"You went from an honors class to a special ed classroom?" Diane leaned in toward Kamau and asked in disbelief. She absolutely could not believe what she was hearing.

"There was no other place for me to go," Kamau said nodding his head, "I mean, I was too … I had already achieved to the point where I was way above regular ed, so the only availability in the school was to take a math class with the special education students who were there, who had aged out. But that's where I met one of my favorite teachers. He also became my godfather. He had an endearing way of reaching the students who were there. He was definitely caring. He took time to listen. He gave us opportunities to reach and teach each other, so if I didn't understand something, I could listen to someone else who was in the classroom and listen to the way they presented it. And I was like *I get it*. He gave us so many opportunities to do that, and he was more of a facilitator than a regular teacher. He just facilitated concepts and thinking and helped us to refine who we were. And before I knew it, I was standing up in the class many times leading a lesson. *He* took my outspokenness, my curiosity and turned it around to be something very positive and affirming." Kamau glanced at Diane and smiled. He had not shared any of this with her before, but he really liked her and trusted her, so he felt comfortable opening up to her.

As Diane looked at Kamau, tears welled up in her eyes, "Good God, Kamau! I'm so sorry that happened to you. But I'm glad that you finally had a teacher who saw the you that I see—brilliant, talented, kind." She caressed the right side of Kamau's face with the back of her left hand.

He looked over at Diane as he pulled the car into a parking space at the Botanical Garden. He took her hand and kissed it, "Thanks, Hun, but I'm okay. I took my challenges to be launching pads for my success." He kissed her hand again, "Without those experiences, I wouldn't be right here with you today." He kissed her on the lips. They both took a deep breath. He was really falling for her, but because she was in school full time in Philly and only in Pittsburgh on some weekends and school breaks, they had promised to take it slow.

"You're really something special. What a beautiful example of resilience and success you are for your students," Diane said, gently caressing Kamau's face with the palm of her hand. She sat back into her seat, "Whew." They could both feel the heat in that car.

Kamau sat back, "Thank you, Diane. I am who I am because of all of that and because of the children. In my experience, the young girls I see—they don't see a lot of positive Black men in their lives; they don't see how a real man is supposed to act, so they tend to actually gravitate towards male teachers like me and follow in our steps. Not in terms of doing what we do, but they watch us, learn from us a little more, like they need a big brother, uncle type of father role model. They look for that within their teachers. And I'm grateful because I don't want them to fall for these knuckleheads and think that's the only thing out there. *He's not in jail; I guess he's the only thing I can choose from.* It's kind of like they don't have much of an example either."

Diane nodded and looked down at her unzipped coat. They bundled up and got out the car. As they walked over to the Garden entrance, Kamau pulled out his phone so the attendant could scan their mobile tickets. As they walked into the Garden, they held gloved hands. From the entrance, they could already see that the lights were incredible.

Diane marveled at the lights. This was her first time visiting the Dazzling Nights experience as well. "You know, I appreciate how you express yourself. I'll keep it 100: most guys I meet are guarded, unwillingly to be transparent about who they are and how they've come to be who they are. But you, you're like an open book." She squeezed his hand and looked into his eyes.

"Self-expression is key for me because I'm also a poet. You can get a lot of emotions and things out in writing of poetry. It's kind of like when you are able to do that verbally as well as written and then you can be yourself. That's what makes kids comfortable around me," Kamau responded.

"Yes, and I love your poetry—so honest and raw, real. I've learned a lot about you from the poetry you've shared with me," Diane remarked.

Kamau was pleased that Diane saw him in that light. He had hoped that he wasn't coming across too "soft," but he found it necessary to be his whole self with her. He felt she deserved that from him. He responded, "Me, I'm just simple. You don't have to wonder what my motives are or what I'm thinking. I'm very upfront with people. I let people know which direction I'm going in, where I'm trying to lead them, and what I'm trying to accomplish because this is just who I am. I want to give people an opportunity to say they're *on this trip with me* or they're not. One thing I don't like people to do with me is to get all the way in with me and then the false pretenses come out. You know what I mean?"

"I totally know what you mean, Kamau," Diane started, "I'm an upfront and honest person with people because, quite frankly, I'm a take it or leave it type person. I'm glad if you love me and you like me, but I'm going to keep it moving if you don't. Life is just too short, and I can't worry about people who don't have my best interest at heart. That's one of the reasons I do the work that I do in the way that I do."

They stopped to admire the interactive lights on the ground that were lighting up with each step they took. Kamau laughed as Diane mimicked Michael Jackson in the Billie Jean video.

"You're hilarious!" Kamau exclaimed. He knew Diane had a great sense of humor, but he had never seen her get so silly before.

"Awww man! I miss MJ so much! He was the man! I mean he was ahead of his time. Everybody wanted to be him," Diane said as she continued to dance on the lights.

Kamau shook his head and responded, "Yeah, I love him to death, but Michael Jackson's life was a tragedy. I wouldn't want his life for anything. He might have had all the money in the world, all the fame, but the man couldn't be himself. He couldn't walk out in the street anytime in his life and just be a normal person because it was always people trying to get at him: take his time, get his autograph, even crazy people that wanted to stalk him and all that. No wonder he died of drugs. He needed every bit of them just to feel like he belonged in this world. There's a lot of people like that. No, I wouldn't want that kind of life for anything, for nothing."

"You said that. And you ain't wrong either," Diane concurred. "So you're a poet and educator, with no aspirations of a more complicated life of fame and stardom." Diane walked in front of Kamau, turned to face him, took both of his hands in hers, and continued walking backward, "What else should I know about you? How does Kamau Miller's life look?"

Kamau looked down at Diane's hands then up at lights in the trees flanking the walkway, "For me it's just simple. I want to keep making sure I stay along the path that God has for me. I've seen too much of how the world looks on people who grow up in the projects. I've been exposed to just about everything. I've had friends that have been killed. I've been robbed, held up at gunpoint. I've had people try to jump me, the whole nine. I've been around drugs. Never took any, never did anything like that. I had a father that absolutely would've killed me if he found out that I did some of these things, but I knew they were around. I have friends that got locked up, people that I grew up with. I've been exposed to everything, but I also grew up with two parents that really put an emphasis on education. I spent most summers with my uncle down south. Even with all that, I was spared *some* of the hardships that other inner-city kids may go through because I got a little taste of what it was like to be a middle-class child. Both parents pushed education, pushed extracurricular activities, pushed sports, and pushed community involvement. Those are the same things I take now and instill in other people's children because being well-rounded is where it is." Kamau gazed at Diane. He added, "I'm a bit of rebel too. I have to say that. Because I have a strong personality, and I'm educated, and I don't have a problem helping people understand that." Diane looked at Kamau and playfully rolled her eyes at his last statement. She was still walking backward. He looked down at her feet. He didn't understand how she could walk backward for so long in those heels.

Kamau inquired, "What about you? How did Diane Rivers become the woman she is today?"

"Heyyyy ... I'm asking the questions here!" Diane stopped walking and poked Kamau in the stomach with her index finger. They laughed. She said, "Nah, I'm kidding with you, Sweetie." She took Kamau's left hand and turned forward so that she could walk beside him again. "Well, I had a father who had a very strong work ethic. My father, it didn't matter, he always was a truck driver, but when he was laid off from working as a truck driver, he worked at Popeye's, so he was dishing up fried chicken. He showed me that no matter what happened, he was gonna do whatever it took to make sure his family had what they needed. My mother worked overnight. She worked from 11 at night to 7 in the morning, came home, made sure we—as children—had what we needed, sent us off to school, went to sleep, was there and made sure the dinner was on before she left. My father ... uhm ... even though he traveled, was, again, a man who was very passionate about making sure the family had what they needed, and that what he said, he meant, but he loved us hard and passionately. It built all of us to be very strong individuals, so in my family unit, I'm a mental health advocate, my mom became a teacher when I graduated high school, my sister works with children in the social services realm. My father, people know him from all over the world and in the country. He gets people together just by cooking, and that's a love that we all have. My brother loves to cook, too. And what does he do? He brings people together just by cooking. That's my family!"

"So your entire clan is about community, getting together, cooking, loving on one another?" Kamau asked.

"Indeed," Diane replied. "I just come from a hard-working people, and I never want to let them down. I am person who cares about people and who wants to help everybody be happy. I feel like people should have a stress-free life or as stress-free as possible, but then at the same time, it's about taking care of business, and sometimes those two things don't go hand in hand. Sometimes when I'm super focused, people think I'm being mean. But when I'm taking care of business, it's never from a mean or hateful standpoint. I just want *everybody* to be okay. You hear me? I'm just out here working hard, trying to get free!" She let go of Kamau's hands and threw both of her hands in the air. She walked ahead of him, turned in a circle, and stretched her arms out wide.

"I see you!" Kamau clapped his hands for his beautiful date.

She turned toward him and asked, "What's freedom look like for you, Kamau?"

Kamau looked up at the stars in the sky and responded, "To me, these kids talk about how much money they want to make. I'm like, 'Is that what your life is going to be consumed with, making money?' I was like, 'Do you know how miserable you're going to be?' Look at all the rich people who can't stay off drugs, who can't leave the alcohol alone, who are in rehab for this or that, who've beaten up their spouse, who are doing all this stuff. It's not because they don't have the money, it's just that they're so isolated from reality that they just don't know how to relate to people." He paused, "I just want people to gravitate towards me in a way where they genuinely love me and have respect for me. That's what I want out of my life. As long as I can pay my bills, and I don't have to live paycheck to paycheck, that's freedom to me. I don't need to be a millionaire in order to be happy. As long as everything that I want and need to take care of is done, my future kids have what they need, that's happiness right there."

"That's happiness indeed," Diane concurred. She stopped walking and pulled him close for a kiss.

Kamau and Diane stood there, in the middle of the Botanical Garden, with shining Christmas lights and music serenading them, looking in one another's eyes. That night, they had gone from the Blackest place in Pittsburgh to the Whitest, but they were glad that they had one another to take this journey with. That night, neither of them spoke of their fear of state-sanctioned violence and the war on Black bodies. They would save that conversation for another day. On this day, they just wanted to feel loved and be hopeful that their bond would continue to grow. It felt so right to both of them. They hugged tightly, breathing deeply, and wished the moment would never end.

CHAPTER 6
Whose World is This?[54]

"Damn, I'm lookin' busted," Kamau said aloud as he peered at himself in the window of La Nacional Check Cashing Store on West 125th Street. Kamau Miller, a 38-year-old third-grade teacher at Derrick Bell Elementary School in Pittsburgh's Hill District, was visiting his younger sister in Harlem, NY, for the Memorial Day weekend and wanted to get a shape-up before hanging out later that night. The barbershop his brother-in-law recommended, Levels, was directly next door to the check cashing spot, and Kamau was pleased to find the shop without much trouble.

As he pushed open the shop door—"It's Yours!"—he heard his favorite artist letting him know what time it was. He smiled and rapped along: "It's mine, it's mine, it's mine. Whose world is this?"[55] The shop owner, Jerry, looked up from the customer he was just finishing up and greeted Kamau with the common head nod that African American men are known for, especially in close circles and places like the barbershop.

Jerry asked, "You want that fade tightened up?" Kamau laughed, realizing that his hair must've looked worse than he thought if Jerry noticed it that quickly.

He replied, "Yeah. Victor sent me. That's my brother-in-law." Jerry was always pleased when his regular customers referred someone new.

He nodded his head, smiled, and said, "Victor's a cool dude. Have a seat. Be with you in a minute." Jerry was the shop owner; he loved Harlem, and he valued his customers. He opened Levels when he was 25—just after he married his high-school sweetheart, and for the past 16 years, he had managed to maintain a strong, positive reputation in the community.

Kamau, known to his Bell Elementary students as Mr. Miller, looked at the long row of chairs along the wall and sat in the end chair closest to the door. He had waited as long as he could for this haircut because he wanted it to be tight for the night's festivities. His boys had been raving about this new lounge in SoHo. Nas' words wafted through the air: "My strength, my son, the star, will be my resurrection," and CNN played on the television. Kamau felt at home, and that felt good. Even though Kamau had missed his home and his friends, this is the first time in 4 years that he had been home or seen his boys. After his first-year teaching, his school district had recruited him to run their summer school program, which took up all his extra time, days off, and most of his summer break. He remembered feeling surprised by how impressed they were by his culturally responsive teaching style, leadership ability, and innovative lessons: he was only doing what he felt would best engage the children. And back in Harlem, he was just a "regular dude."

While he sat waiting for his cut, he thought about his students. His mind wandered as he wondered what they were doing this weekend. He hoped they were safe, especially Mikhail. Mikhail was a little Black boy who was in another third-grade class. Like Mr. Miller, Mikhail had moved to Pittsburgh from New York but was from Brooklyn, and he had a Brooklyn attitude. Kamau laughed to himself as he recalled this academic year with Mikhail. That little dude didn't take nothing off nobody; if you said something to him, he punched you in your mouth. You got too close to him, he'd tell you to get away from him. If you didn't, he punched you in the mouth. And that's just not New York because that's also how they were brought up in the Hill. If they don't leave you alone, then you hit them and make them leave you alone. So Kamau couldn't be mad at Mikhail for doing what he was taught. However, at the same time, he needed someone to whom he could talk to keep himself out of trouble. And the White teachers, they didn't know how to talk to him, didn't know how to handle him. Kamau knew that if he wanted to help

Mikhail, then he needed to develop a rapport with him; Kamau needed to value the cultural capital that Mikhail brings to the classroom and appreciate him for who he is. Therefore, he listened to Mikhail speak, and he found ways to relate to the things about which he spoke; most importantly, every day, he was patient with him and encouraged him to be successful.

Every morning, Mikhail would come to Mr. Miller's room: "What's up Mr. Miller? What's going on?"

Kamau would shake his hand and give him a hug. He'd talk to him a little bit, like "We're gonna have a good day today—no incidents." Then, he would let Mikhail's teacher know that if he were getting off task or behaving too badly to send him to Mr. Miller's classroom: "I'll talk to him for you, calm him down, send him back, or what not, or he can just stay. We're doing the same things in our class anyway."

Kamau found it important to connect with his students—especially the Black boys because he felt that they needed role models. They needed to see positive images of Black men in positions of authority and power—not just rappers or athletes. He wanted his students to believe that school was a safe and empowering place for them.

Lost in his thoughts, Kamau didn't hear Jerry calling him, "Hey, my man! You still want this cut?"

Kamau, snapped back to Harlem and smiled, "Of course! Of course. My bad Man, I was just thinking about my kids back in The Hill." Kamau stood up, walked toward Jerry's chair, made himself comfortable, and placed his "order": "Could you fade it up to here?" Kamau pointed to about 1 inch above his ear. "Leave the length on the top and fade it all the way bald. Edge it up all the way around but leave a natural front."

"Yep … so what's The Hill?" Jerry responded as he draped a black barber's cape over Kamau's body and snapped it behind his neck.

Kamau replied, "The Hill District—in Pittsburgh. I'm a teacher out there." Kamau had piqued the interest of several of the other men in the shop by saying he was a teacher.

"A teacher? What you teach, man?" asked Slim, looking up from sweeping. Slim was a short, stocky, caramel-complected brother. He had been cutting hair at Levels, off and on, for almost 10 years. Slim had turned

50 years old the month before and prided himself on having escaped being "locked down" (married) for so long.

"I'm a third-grade teacher," Kamau replied.

Slim stopped sweeping for a minute, stood the broom upright, and leaned on the top of the broomstick. "How'd you get into that?" he asked.

Kamau thought for a second and responded, "Well, I used to tutor and stuff when I was young. But I thought I wanted to be a businessman, so I was studying Business Administration at BMCC (Borough of Manhattan Community College), and a girl I was dating asked me if I wanted to volunteer at an afterschool program where she worked. I gave it a shot, and I couldn't deny how much I loved working with the kids. The thing is … I just couldn't ignore that the Black boys didn't have nobody to look up to. I mean they have the sistas, but they don't have no brothers to relate to, nobody that looked like them in the schools—except the janitor." Slim looked down at his broom, and Kamau added, "and that's cool. That's honorable work, but they didn't have no … no Black men to help teach them in a way they could understand. I mean, these boys were ALWAYS getting in trouble. So … I figured I'd give education a shot, and I transferred to Hunter College and did the QUEST program."

"So now that you're there, are they still getting in trouble?" Jerry asked, switching clippers.

Kamau laughed, "Yeah, they still get in trouble sometimes, but I think I make a difference. Most of these boys from The Hill are like boys here in Harlem. They running the streets. They don't know their daddies. Their mommas are working hard, trying to teach these boys to be men, but it's hard. Then, they go to school mad and act out because they ain't got no daddies there either—just more sistas and lots of White women telling them what to do. And when they just try to be themselves, they get in trouble!" Kamau frowned and waved his hand in a frustrated motion, then continued, "Maaaaaaaaaannnnn … I've seen it all: these boys being referred for Special Ed left and right because they won't sit still for four hours!"

"Hmpf! Slim can't sit still for 4 min! Maybe he needs some Special Ed!" Jerry teased. The barbershop erupted with laughter.

"Alright Jerry!" Slim said, pointing his broomstick in Jerry's direction, shaking his head, and laughing. He propped the broom against his station, sat down in his own chair, and turned to face Kamau. "Watch me sit."

Kamau laughed and continued, "A lot of the things that boys do I can catch, and I say, 'Oh, he's just being a boy'. And female teachers get on me all the time because they want to jump down a boy's throat some times for things that they are doing or saying or commenting on. I just don't jump on them like that, and the White teachers say, 'Aren't you going to get on them about such and such?' and I'm like, 'No. He's just being a boy. He just told you he thought the girl was pretty: just saying it in his own way'. For example, a boy the other day came up to me saying he really liked this one particular girl. He was like, 'Man, look at her; she's pretty, and she got a nice butt', and the teachers were jumping all down him like he offended her, and I was saying, 'Calm down'. I mean, he is allowed to be a boy. I mean what you want him to say? Ya know … this is elementary. He's a fifth grader."

Slim throws his head back laughing, then says, "How you deal with that man? If I had a little daughter, and she told me some boy was looking at her butt, I'd be up at that school wringing his neck! Y'all lucky I ain't got no kids!"

"Yes, we're ALL lucky you don't have any kids Slim. The world is a better place because there's only one of you!" Jerry retorted, and then continued, "So Teach, you trying to say that you try to make a space for boys to be boys, right?"

"Exactly!" Kamau replied, "I'm just saying, I don't get on them for the harmless stuff. He didn't touch her butt. He didn't cross that line. He talked to me—Black boy to Black man. I try to be somebody that they can feel comfortable with and able to talk to about any situation. Then, when the time comes to educate them on when and what to do and not to say, I can do that better than somebody who fusses at them for everything because if I get on them about everything, then they won't tell me anything. I won't know anything; and then, I can't prevent anything. But for his commenting on some girl and how pretty she is, I can't get mad at him for that. But some teachers don't know how to handle that because all they see is sex, and at the end of the day, it's just a little boy crushing; that's all it is. They treat these little Black boys like they grown men. They call that adultification. They adultify these boys—making the little boy things they do into grown men actions. Then, they punish them—make them out to be criminals for little boy behaviors."

"They ADULTIFY them. That's sick man. Boys gotta be allowed to be boys," Slim adds—still sitting in his chair.

Kamau asserts, "Yeah, Man. I try to give them space to be themselves, and, at the same time, feel a connection to someone. I wanted to be able to create an environment for the kids where they felt connected, cared for, and capable. Right now, I have a class that, if I had a child, I would want me teaching my kid. I talk to the kids. I let them know there's nothing wrong with who they are and where they're from. I incorporate their names and the names of their neighborhood streets into the math word problems; I encourage them to talk about what's going on in the Hill and how they're dealing with stuff. We work out solutions to their real problems and make connections to the stuff we're reading. You feel me? I show them that they are the same as the kids in the books they're reading and that they live in the same world that we study in science and social studies. I do this because I believe that if you have a kid that's connected to you, and you have a kid that believes that he is capable of doing the work, that's half the battle. They work harder, and they achieve more because they don't feel so beat down all the time."

"Ahhhhhh! That's what's up." Jerry started, "Do you see this adultification with the White boys, too? I have three sons, and they're always complaining that the White boys get away with murder."

Kamau asserted, "I definitely see all boys struggling, but the Black boys—The Hill is 99% Black—and they are struggling like no other! They make up the majority of Special Education; they're suspended from school more than any other, and they drop out of high school more than any other population. The only group even close to Black boys is Latino boys. They're suffering, too, you know." Kamau stops and sighs, then continues, "In all honesty a lot of these children only have the males they see in videos and hear on the radio to guide them, so we as Black men need to show our youngsters there's more to life than being a gangsta' and making drug money. Show them it's not cool to go to jail. I be teaching my students about Nas and the greats like him. I try to school them and challenge them to listen to artists who don't just glorify negative things in their lyrics."

"You use HipHop in your class out there in Pittsburgh?!" Slim interrupted Kamau. He was sitting on the edge of his chair, but he was still sitting.

Kamau replied, "Oh yeah! HipHop is about self-expression, self-respect and awareness—always has been. The English language is the hardest to learn in the world, and because our words can have so many different meanings, context dictates the message that is being conveyed. The world tried to ignore HipHop because it came from us. It was in a vernacular that the masses could not follow, but how is that any different from the drums, calls, songs, and chants of our ancestors? It's not just about rhyming; it is about educating and mentoring, so I use slang, HipHop terminology, and all types of figurative language to get points across in my curriculum. I use HipHop songs to teach grammar and poetry. I use imagery to connect urban life, suburban life, and education. It helps the students to express themselves in ways and terms that are beneficial to them. I mean … I think that we spend too much time trying to make our youth into what we want them to be and not what they want to be and what they are good at. My mother used to always tell me that Proverbs 22:6 says that we are to train up the children in the ways that they should go. They need to be taught, supported, and guided in how to put their particular gifts and talents to use in this world." Kamau paused. "You know …, what is cool to these kids is that I listen to them. Once I have them, they do anything that I ask them to do because they know I see them, and I care about them."

"Teach here is schooling you today, huh Slim?" Jerry directed his compliment and question to his colleague and longtime friend. Slim grinned and sat back in his chair. Kamau looked down at his phone, smiled, and thought how Victor must've known that Kamau would enjoy this shop because he knew Jerry and Slim would be so cool to talk to. Just then, Nas' "Queens, Get the Money" started playing.

Kamau looked up, "Maaaaaaaannnn, this is my jam right here! For real, this cut inspires me to keep doing what I do every day!" Slim and Jerry listened closely, and Kamau rapped along. "That part right there! When he says 'I'll be his daddy if there's nobody there to love it'.[56] I feel like that EVERY DAY! I'll be their father if I have to. As a matter of fact, it hit me a few weeks ago: one of the young men in my class came up to me and was like, 'Mr. Miller, you know what my momma said? She said you like a father here at the school—that you take care of all the young Black boys. Mr. Miller, you our father at school?' I was like, 'Well, uh I ain't never think about it like that, but I mean, I'm whatever I gotta be'. I'm saying some of them don't have fathers, some don't have bigger brothers, some don't have uncles, some don't have whatever they need to get them through. So I mean, if it's a listening ear, or whatever male position they're lacking in life, I take on that position. Even to the point if they're not lacking anything: well I'm their teacher, and I'm usually their first Black male teacher. So I mean, whatever I gotta be, I'm step up and be it to help them get through whatever they need to get through, and even more importantly, to help shape them for the future. I have to make sure they're prepared to go out in this cold world, do their best, and shine. You know what I'm saying?"

Jerry asserted, "Yeah man. That's why I stay committed to my wife and sons. But I know a lot of dudes who ain't though." Jerry looks out the window for a brief moment as if he is lost in a moment of deep reflection. Then, he adds, "You know, I read this article the other day in *Vibe* about something called 'Otherfathering', and I could totally relate. It sounds like what you're talking about. The article said that otherfathers are men who provide guidance, mentoring, and support to young dudes as they grow into men. I do know some oldheads that do that for young cats. They try to expose them to what's going on in the real world, talk to them, keep it 100 with them. Black youth need to be exposed to the real world. They can't just be in this little bubble, thinking that the real world is as nice and comfy as the school building is. I think teachers do kids a disservice to not teach them about some of the things that they will see in life, ya know, try to shed light on how things are in the real world." He shakes his head, "I teach my sons that this world is tough, and there ain't no love in it for the Black man, so we gotta make our own way. We gotta learn the game, play it a little 'til we get what we need, and then do our own thing. That's the only way we'll be successful and be able to take care of our own."

"You are so right, Jerry! I work hard to stay relevant to my students. I listen to the music they listen to, and I give them the space to be themselves without judgement and with love. I create a safe space—a welcome space—for them. I pay close attention to where they are developmentally, and I provide them with activities and support that can take them to the next level. They learn the curriculum, but they also learn about the real world. I have some great mentor teachers in my school who give me dope tips on how to give my kids the best learning experiences, but then I add my HipHop touch to all of that, and instruction becomes relevant. It becomes authentic. It becomes real to them, you know what I mean? I also go to the rec center to support them in their athletic events. I try to show them that they matter, and that they're so much more than just students to me: they're human beings, and they can be whoever they want to be in this world." Kamau explains and then raps, "The world is yours. The world is yours!" The men laugh, and Slim gets up and gives Kamau a five.

"We need more brothers to be teachers like you, Teach," Slim added, "You're alright with me." He grabs his broom and resumes sweeping.

Kamau looked down at his phone again and grinned. This time spent at Levels has been a long time coming. He felt good about being able to build with other Black men, and as Jerry removed the cape from his shoulders, and handed him a hand mirror, he felt even better about looking good for his night with his friends.

"It's tight, Jerry. Thanks. What do I owe you?" Kamau asked, pulling his wallet out of his pocket.

Jerry hung up the barber's cape and waved at Kamau. "Your money's no good here, Teach. You just keep doing what you're doing—keep taking care of our boys."

Kamau smiled at Jerry and shook his hand. "I can handle that. Thanks Jerry. I'll be sure to tell Victor how you hooked me up."

Kamau Miller walked out of Levels, and as he turned the corner, he heard a police siren and saw two police officers running toward him. He immediately stopped in his tracks and threw his hands up. Then, he saw two Black teenagers run around the corner across the street, and the officers and a police car sped after them. Kamau shook his head, put his hands down, dug them deep into his pockets, and continued walking back to his sister's apartment. As he walked down the crowded street, he could hear that same question he was so hyped to hear less than an hour ago, "Whose world is this?" This time, Kamau didn't smile. He didn't even answer.

CHAPTER 7
The Elementary School Was Where I Needed to Be

"Hey, my Mans!" Kamau threw back his right hand and gave Adam dap as they embraced. "Where's your boy?" Kamau glanced around the dimly lit lounge, not seeing Terence with Adam as he had expected.

Nodding his head toward a busy section of the room over Kamau's left shoulder, Adam replied, "He's at the bar. He saw his ex over there, and he's tripping."

Kamau laughed, shook his head, and looked toward the couches, "He needs to leave that girl alone. Where's our spot?" The friends had been planning this outing for several weeks, and after the interesting afternoon he spent at Levels, Kamau was looking forward to this opportunity to unwind while having some grown man fun. Having heard how packed this Scotch & Cigars Party can get, Adam had reserved a table.

"We're right there." Adam led Kamau to the right side of the room to a large, black rectangular table with an 8-inch-tall black pillar candle in the center. The lit candle was flanked by three black Cohiba ashtrays—each waiting for a cigar—and three black coasters—each ready for an on the rocks glass—to complete the vibe. There was a black leather couch large enough to seat three people behind the table and two black leather armchairs in front of the table.

"Everything in here really is black, huh?" Kamau asked gazing around the room in amazement. Adam was a regular at Blk Swan in the SoHo area of lower Manhattan, and he had been bragging about the laid-back adult crowd, the smooth ambience, and the all-black décor. But this was Kamau's first time here, so he was taking it all in as he made himself comfortable on the couch.

"This your first time?" Kamau was slightly startled by the deep voice. Caught up in the newness of the all-black space, he had not noticed the gentleman sitting in a black leather recliner to the left of their table.

Kamau laughed, "Is it that obvious?" The gentleman—dressed in a maroon seersucker suit, crisp white button-up shirt, and black wing tips—took a sip of his drink, glanced at Kamau from under his black trilby, and smiled, "Yeah. I see you looking all around. But it's all good. They went all out with the black theme. The ladies love it." He tipped his glass toward a group of beautifully dressed Black women dancing and laughing on the dance floor.

"That's what's up." Kamau replied, admiring the ladies. "What's good here?" Kamau asked, pointing to the gentleman's drink.

"Hmm … they've got all the good stuff. This is Macallan 18: my personal fave. But you have to try the Glenlivet 12. It's right. Pairs nicely with cigars," The gentleman responded.

As Kamau was getting drink suggestions from his new friend, Terence and Adam joined him at the table. Coincidently, Terence had a bottle of Glenlivet 12 in one hand and 3 on the rocks glasses in the other. Adam lay 3 Opus X cigars on the table—2 Habanos and 1 Connecticut, and he and Terence sat in the armchairs across from their friend. "What's up, Man?" They both greeted the gentleman in the recliner.

"Hey there, Gentlemen. I'm Foster Hackney." He stood up, extended his hand, and shook each of the three friends' hands. The friends introduced themselves, and Foster asked, "Enjoying the event so far?"

"Yeah. It's nice." Terence responded, "Our mans is in town, so we wanted to get him out the house and around some other adults." He laughed.

Foster chuckled and turned to Kamau, "Cool. How many kids you have?"

Kamau smiled and replied, "26." Foster raised his thick eyebrows, opened his eyes wide, and looked at Kamau waiting for more details.

Terence and Adam laughed. Kamau added, "I'm an elementary school teacher. I teach third grade out in PA."

"Oh, that's interesting. How long you been doing that? Do you enjoy it?" Foster asked, genuinely interested.

"I've been teaching for 5 years, and I completely love it. What about you?" Kamau returned.

"I'm an insurance underwriter … for just over a year now … and hmmm … it definitely pays the bills, but I can't say that I love it," Foster replied, appearing deep in thought. He had been pondering a career change for some time now, but he was not sure if he really wanted to take the leap; plus, his current job nicely supported his lifestyle, and it kept his wife happy (she was one of the women on the dance floor). He asked, "Did you always know you wanted to be a teacher?"

Kamau sipped the scotch Terence had poured him and sat forward on the couch, "Bro, a lot of men don't get into teaching by starting off saying 'I'm gonna be a teacher'. Many of us started off trying to do something else, and then we just fell into teaching because it was something that we could do, and I'm a victim of that myself. I was studying Business Administration, and then, I started volunteering with kids, and the rest is history."

"Is that right?" Foster slowly picked up his Ashton maduro cigar and lit it using a kissing motion. He took a slow drag and opened up, "Ya know, when I was in college, I used to do some volunteer work with a friend of mine during the summer. I worked with middle school kids at different camps, and I could relate to them. This older lady worked there. She was a retired teacher, and she talked me into coming back the next semester to do more volunteer work and be a Big Brother. I was a Big Brother for a couple of years to one of the kids there and had an opportunity to find out the kind of things he was going through and help guide him in a way to get him away from some of the same stuff that I was dealing with when I was his age—12–13 years old."

"Yeah man," Kamau replied. He decided to join Foster by lighting one of the Habanos Adam had brought to the table a few moments ago. "Real talk: I felt that it was God pushing me towards education. When I started to *really* enjoy working with the children, I was like 'Oh. Okay, well I guess ... this is a sign from above'. Because, I mean, before then, I was really trying not to go into education. I was studying business because I really didn't want to teach. But when I started volunteering with those kids, I started praying about it, and then the scripture came to me: 'Raise up a child in the way they should go' [Proverbs 22:6]."

Adam interrupted, "Ohhh boy, your mans over here quoting scripture." He tapped Terence on his arm, but Terence wasn't listening to the conversation. He was facing the bar, trying to pretend that he wasn't observing his ex as she laughed, danced, and sipped scotch with her friends.

Terence took a drag of the other Habano and said, "Huh?"

"Forget it, Man." Adam shook his head and added, "it's definitely a profession that you have to want and be called to do ..." he shook his head, "but can we lay off the scripture? I'm not trying to be Holy in here tonight." Adam picked up the Connecticut cigar, pulled a torch lighter out his pocket, and lit his cigar.

Kamau laughed, waved his hand at his friend, and turned back to Foster, "So I was like, 'Okay, well I'll just do this', and I kinda just jumped in, not knowing exactly where I wanted to go, but it just felt right. God just ordered all my steps from that point. You feel me?"

"Yeah. I do." Foster sat back for a second, and the two men were quiet. Adam and Terence, knowing how much their friend loved to talk about teaching, walked out onto the dance floor and started dancing with the group of ladies Foster had pointed out earlier. One of the women, Foster's wife, looked back at her husband. He nodded his head and tipped his hat at her as an indication that he was comfortable with her new dance partners. Foster enjoyed the vibe and the ambience at Blk Swan, but he wasn't much of a dancer: that was his lady's forte. Comfortable with their individual personalities and secure in their marriage, their evenings at Blk Swan were often spent with him at a table, chilling with a cigar and scotch, and her on the dance floor, getting her groove on until her feet and legs hurt.

Foster turned to Kamau and said thoughtfully, "For me, school was always just something to do because it was something I had to do. I never really understood the main purpose of it. When I was younger, my mother got me involved in Pop Warner Football, and the football coach—African-American man—he helped push me. What I mean by that is throughout my life, there's been people: I can remember being in the 5th grade, and I had a teacher that said, 'If you go pick pecans off this tree for me, I will pay for your field trip'. Uhm … and I remember being in the 6th grade, there was this old cat that did landscaping. One day, I went to his yard because I had seen this young cat working there, and I said, 'Hey, can I work here, too?' He called me two weeks later, and we're having a conversation, and he offered me a job to work there."

Foster paused and looked out at the dance floor. He took a drag of his cigar and continued, "There have always been people who kind of were staggered throughout my life, teaching me invaluable life lessons, and I never picked up on this … until now. Hmpf. I like to think of them as *Merchants of Hope*. I heard about that term, 'Merchants of Hope', some years ago in a video by this woman named Crystal … Kuykendall, I believe, and it resonated with me, so I've never forgotten it. Because of those Merchants of Hope in my life, I was able to get to where I am today. And if we remove any of those individuals, my life could be crazy. I could be the uhm … megamind behind some kind of drug enterprise or something because that's the path I could've easily been down had I not had these people in my life."

Kamau got excited, "Yo! I feel you on that, Son! I've had people in my life like that, and I just want to be able to offer what those people have offered to me. I think that's really, at this point in life, the reason I do what I do … because someone else did it for me. I think that if we just harness those great things that others have done for us and do it for other people, then I think that's really the way to change the world. And so … that's the inspiration that I get behind what I do. For me, it was later found. It's almost like you go through the experience, and then you find after you've been through it versus, you know, you just knew. I'm not one of those people who just knew from kindergarten that they always wanted to be a teacher, and they played school. Mine was like God put me in these places to grow and to learn and to shape my life and because of that, I'm giving back—only what's been given to me. I think my life experiences are probably the most indirect and unique qualifier for me to do what I do."

Foster recounted, "I feel that. In high school, I was in JROTC, and I had an opportunity to develop some leadership skills. I became a part of a drill team and the Color Guard, and I moved up in rank quickly: second lieutenant colonel then first sergeant major. I even got the opportunity in my senior year to go mentor some fourth graders at an elementary school. Those little kids were something! But that's a long story. Did you ever think of teaching bigger kids? Like middle or high school, ya know, teenagers? I'm not sure I wanna teach anybody's little rug rat kid, getting on my nerves all day long." Foster laughed and tended to his cigar.

Kamau puffed his cigar, then replied, "When I went to school, everything I did, all of my research, all of my observations, student teaching, everything was done at the elementary school level, and I just fell in love with the little kids. Like, at first, I thought I didn't want to because they're little and they cry and they whine and all that stuff. I wanted someone I could talk to and be like 'Sit down. Do what you're supposed to do', and they understand. But as long I don't go lower than 3rd grade, I'm fine. Like 3rd grade was the lowest I worked with, and they don't do as much crying; they are able to hold themselves together. I did 4th grade for my student teaching, and I loved it. I haven't taught middle school, but one thing I know is very different is that in elementary, you have to balance a myriad of learning styles and a pace that has to be spread over 5 different subjects. The amount of content knowledge that is necessary for elementary teachers across the board increases the workload. Whereas in middle and high, at least you have it scaled down to one subject, and kids are recommended to be in classes that should fit their pace. You can put more of the accountability on them. But in elementary school, because the kids are younger, you have to tread the fine line between encouragement and accountability."

Kamau felt his phone vibrate. He looked down at his phone and glanced at a sweet but brief text from Diane. She had stayed in Philly for the long weekend to work on a research project with her faculty advisor. He smiled, replied with an eyes emoji, and put his phone back into his pocket. He missed her, but he wanted to be present for this conversation. He admired the length of the ash on his cigar, smiled at Foster, and continued, "Plus, from my observations, I felt the elementary school was where I needed to be. I do it for the purpose of helping a kid at an earlier age. I think we have all tried doing it at the high school route. Though it does help a lot of kids at the last gate ..., but what if more of us hit them early on with the mindset and got it right for them then instead of them having to figure out who they are or what they are about when they're almost done with school? By that point, we have lost the war" Kamau shrugged, "or many of the battles. It's such a critically sensitive time period. They have an opportunity to get on the right path from the start, whereas in middle school or high ... I mean it's not too late for them. But they just start getting to the point when they're set in their ways. Elementary school is just one of the places where you can help mold those kids a little bit more." At that moment, Kamau noticed Adam at the bar, waving for him to come over. Kamau nodded.

"I can feel that" Foster started, "this idea of molding kids."

Kamau interrupted, "Hold that thought, Bro. I'll be right back." Kamau walked over to the bar where his friend was standing. The bar was crowded. Frustrated with trying to get the bartender's attention, Adam decided to check in with his friend in the meantime.

Adam asked, "Hey man. You good? I see you made a friend." Adam nodded his head toward Foster, "You don't want to join us?" Adam nodded his head toward the dance floor where Terence was dancing in the middle of a circle of women.

Kamau responded, "Nah, I'm good. The dude is really cool. We've been talking about—"

Adam interrupted, "Let me guess: *teaching!*" Kamau shoved Adam's right shoulder, and the two friends laughed. "Yo, real talk: I know you luh the kids," Adam imitated Martin Lawrence, "but what about the single moms? That's got to be the thing keeping your nose so open for teaching, right?"

Kamau laughed, "Yeah, the single moms, man, that's the best perk." Kamau shook his head, "Nah, I'm just teasing. Y'all always say that. I'm tryna mold minds, and you guys out here like, *You be hollering at the students' moms?* And every time, I be like, *Man, no. It's not like that alright.* For one, the parents that come to see me are not happy. They're already mad. You don't have a chance to holler at them. I just enjoy what I do, I have a good time. Kids are funny. The staff is funny. Mr. Nasir, he's the janitor. He's hilarious."

Adam shook his head, "I'm asking you about women, and you over here talking about Mr. Nasir." Then, Adam tapped Kamau on his arm, "Yo! Guess who I just saw over there!"

Kamau asked, "Who?"

"Divan!" Adam answered.

"Word? I haven't seen her since high school. How she look?" Kamau cupped his hand in front of his mouth and looked around the lounge, "You used to love you some Divan back in the day! Back in Beta Club, her and her crew used to get away with murder!"

"She's looking good," said Adam nodding, "Weren't you in AG[57] with her?"

Kamau sucked his teeth and responded, "Your memory bad? Well, for one, remember, they never expected us Black kids from Frederick Douglass to pass, and so we didn't get the opportunities to go into AG. I never got anything less than a B from kindergarten up and through 6th grade, but not once was I tested to go into AG. Not once were my parents brought in to say that *He may possibly be in AG*. And I was in the top 5 in math from 4th grade up, through 7th grade, but still it never happened."

"Right, right," Adam replied, "You remember when I got into Beta Club and then Divan made it? Her dad is Black, and her mom is white, right? Uhmm. And then, … the other Black girls … there weren't that many … in school with us. I wanna say that there were maybe 6 Black people period …. yeah … it was me." He counted six other names on his fingers. "Yeah, there was 6 of us, and Divan and Shirley were the only two girls. Divan, she got, she got away with murder though. She could do whatever she wanted—honestly. I mean, she was a cute girl, so I don't know if that had anything to do with it or not."

Kamau laughed, "You know it did." Kamau puffed his cigar.

Adam nodded in agreement and continued, "But she could do whatever she wanted, and she was always—I mean she did have good grades—but she was also able to go into AG. I finally got into the Beta Club when I was in, like, 8th grade, but it was too late to really be active then because I was getting ready to go to high school. Remember, the National Honor Society was something else? You had to pay money and all this other stuff, right?"

Kamau nodded, "Yeah, you wasn't gonna do that." He laughed.

Adam added, "Nope. But in high school, there was girls from other middle schools there, too. Shakena, she was ... Shakena was real bright. She was smarter than I was. I can say that, and she went off to Hofstra. Me and Divan were the same. Our grades were identical all through school. That's why it used to burn me up sometimes because she got away with murder, whereas, if I did something, I got called on it. I couldn't get away—I couldn't do anything remotely off-task, and I'd get caught, but then my cousins that I hung with and my friends." Adam looked sternly at Kamau, "You guys were troublemakers, so the eyes were already watching us anyway."

Kamau grabbed his heart as if Adam's accusation hurt his feelings.

"Yeah," Adam continued, "Deborah, she was the other Black girl. Her grades were lower than me and Divan both, but she was a cheerleader, so she got away with a few things, too. It's like, in high school, there weren't really get any advantages to being AG kids or in AP classes, so I didn't sign up for any of those because I didn't want that extra work. And I was playing sports, so I didn't need all that ..." Adam thought for a second, "And I had to work. Uhm ... I think Deborah might've had some AP classes and Divan as well. Shakena, she had all the—she comes from like the all-American family, ya know, both parents with a house. They had good jobs, so she had everything. She didn't have to work. She didn't play any sports in school, and she was good in school, so she got what she wanted." Terence, catching the tail end of Adam's last statement, asked, "You guys talking about Deborah?"

"Not *that* Deborah, the one we went to school with," Adam laughed at Terence. Terence's ex-girlfriend's name was also Deborah, and he had been quietly, but obviously obsessing over her all night. While hanging with Adam, he had been trying not to watch her enjoy herself without him.

Terence watched Deborah across the dance floor. She was on the opposite side of the lounge smoking a cigar with her best friend and a White guy that Terence had never seen before. He narrowed his eyes and said, "If you have to give, you should give freely. Even if you think that it's something that others might not appreciate, give it anyway. Don't give reluctantly and certainly don't give the worst of what you have. You should share with people your spoils, the things that are good to you. If you have something that's good, then share it with somebody else and not give them anything less than what you would want people to give you. That's how I lead my life and I pattern my life."

Kamau and Adam looked at one another with raised eyebrows and looked at Terence. He took a sip of his scotch and continued, "I treat people how I would like to be treated. When I'm not treated a certain way, I'm one to voice that to people like, *Hey, that's not what I would do to you. Could you treat me a little better?* My thing is … and I'm one of those people if I'm in a store and I handed my money to you in your hand, handed my card to you in your hand and then you slide it back on the table, *Did I not pay you enough respect to put that in your hand?* They were like, *Oh I'm sorry, I'm sorry.* I'm just like yes; I want the same respect in return. You feel me?"

Adam and Kamau were confused about what Terence was talking about, but sure that his rambling was about his ex-girlfriend, the two muttered, "Sure."

Terence nodded, still watching Deborah and her companions, "Although some people generally don't do that on purpose, some people do that on purpose because they don't want to touch your hands. Especially when you talk about Caucasian people sometimes." He raised his glass to Deborah's White male companion and winked at his two friends, "Those are the ones that I really like to fire up. I'm like, *Look, do you have a problem? Because if you can't give me back the way that I gave you, then I'll go to another store. You're not the only store in town.* People will quickly snap up and apologize for what they do, but I can tell the ones who are malicious with it and the ones that aren't. The thing is, I get my point across because you're going to put this back in my hand and treat me with the same respect that I gave you. Respect to me is pinnacle in this life. You've got to respect your neighbor. You've got to love your neighbor. No, we don't have to be friends. I don't even have to like you, but the God that I serve says that I get my blessing, I get the fruits of my labor, I get my spiritual beliefs and understandings from the fact that I can be kind to someone else, even if you don't feel the same way towards me. Really my relationship with the Lord is not about anybody else. It's about me. You and I can be the worst of enemies, but I'm going to say good morning to you. I'm going to still say goodbye. If you've got a flat tire and I'm leaving and I see you out there, I'm going to help you change it. That's the type of person that I am. Then I say, *God bless you.* I might even say, *Yes, I know you don't care for me very much but it's my pleasure to help you out.* I'm that person. I know sometimes I shouldn't be. I know me: I like to kind of poke at people sometimes when I know that I'm doing something for them that I know they wouldn't do for me. I kind of salt on them a little bit. I just kind of want to give people something to think about because I want you to remember that I didn't have to, but I did. The reason why I did it is my last thing that I say to you, *God bless you.* That's why I did it. I'm not forcing anything on anybody. I'm telling you like I told you earlier. I'm telling you, *This is my stance. This is what I believe. This is what I'm going to put forth. If that's not something that you agree with, then keep on walking.* You feel me?" Terence looked back at his friends who were staring blankly at him.

Kamau asked, "Yo, you aight, man? You just said a whole lot, and I'm not even sure what you said." Kamau put his left hand on his friend's left shoulder.

Terence took another sip of his drink, looked at Kamau and admitted, "Yeah ... Nah ... I don't know man. This girl got me messed up."

Kamau put his arm around his friend's shoulders and pulled him in for a hug. "You gonna be aight, man. You talk to her?"

"Nope!" Adam intervened, "and he's not going to. Not today. I've ordered our drinks, and we're going back over to entertain these lovely ladies who have been giving us all the love tonight. Right, Terence?" Adam put his hand on his friend's right shoulder and directed him to walk with him back toward the ladies. They were sitting at a table and were dancing and laughing in their seats. As the two walked away, Adam looked back at Kamau and mouthed, "I'll fill you in later. You joining us?"

Kamau nodded his head, which was swirling from the two totally different interactions: the conversation with Adam and Terence's ramble. He said to Adam, "Let me go finish this conversation. I'll be right over."

Kamau walked back over to his seat next to Foster, sat down, took a deep breath, and said, "Hey man. I'm back. We were talking about molding kids." Kamau sat back on the couch, "So what's that long story? I got time." Kamau had been greatly enjoying this conversation with Foster. At the same time, he was also watching Adam and Terence, who had danced their way over to the other side of the room. They were sitting with the group of women, and the round of drinks Adam had ordered, just arrived. Terence looked better, and they seemed to be having a great time. Kamau loved seeing his friends experience joy.

Foster was silent for a moment. He admired his wife's free spirit and infectious energy. She made friends wherever she went, and the dance floor was her playground. Foster was a bit more reserved. He didn't know Kamau at all before today. However, he felt a kinship with him. He enjoyed engaging in high-quality debate and conversation with other Black men like himself, but this was getting deep, and he wasn't sure how much he should share. He wasn't sure how much he *could* share ... and still enjoy the night. A myriad of thoughts swirling around his mind, he shook his head and laughed. Then, his face became serious. He almost seemed to frown, "When I was in JROTC, my sergeant used to tell me that kids just loved to see me do stuff. At that time, it was performing for me, but other people were like, 'Kids just gravitate to you. They listen to you so well'. I had even been working with my younger brother since I was able to drive: we didn't stay in the same household, so I would pick him up and just teach him everything I could, and I knew to try to help him have a better life because we were born into struggle. But one day after school, I remember the principal coming to me because I had just got me a little truck. I was so excited; I worked so hard for that truck. And the principal told me that I couldn't go mentor the kids because—he said my music in my truck was too loud, and I was extremely offended because I was poor. I had a little truck, and I had little, small speakers, and there were other guys with booming sound systems, and I knew for a fact that it wasn't me. But I got suspended, and he told me that I was not a good enough role model for these kids. And I'm thinking, 'I've never been suspended in my entire life, so for this to happen—I mean I don't even have a track record'. I'm thinking, 'if you would just look at my track record as a student, you would see that this doesn't line up. I don't even get a slap on the wrist or anything. You just wanna go suspend me, kick me out of school because you think I'm such a hazard?' That made me wanna say, 'Look, there's no way in the world that you're gonna tell me that I can't be useful to these kids'. But that was the turning point for me. It just turned me off to the thought of teaching."

Just as Foster was finishing his thought, the deejay mixed in "You Must Learn" by KRS-One.[58] Kamau and Foster look at one another, raise their glasses to one another, rest their drinks, stand up, and rap along. Out on the dance floor, Foster noticed his wife, Tiffany, rapping along as well. She and the entire dance floor had their hands in the air shouting the lyrics.

Watching his beautiful Black wife in this beautiful Black space, Foster thought about his Black family—his brother, his children. He thought about other people's children. He could not help but feel a sincere compulsion to do something different—to prove that principal wrong after all these years. What are the chances of meeting a Black male teacher at this party, having this deep conversation, *and* The Teacha[59] being spun in at this moment? After the song ended, he turned to Kamau and shared, "Ya know, I do believe that I have a Biblical responsibility to care for others. If I do not take time to give back and to make giving back a normal part of my life, then I am pretty much a useless human being." He laughs, then continues, "I just know that God did not put me on this earth to be selfish."

Kamau looked at his new friend and declared, "Brother, you do whatever God has put in your heart to do. Stay true to your calling. Do it the right way, and nobody can deny you that."

Tiffany, eager for a quick smoke break, danced over to her husband. Foster grooved with her for a second. So many thoughts were going through his mind, and Tiffany would tell. She raised her right eyebrow at him as her eyes searched her lover's face for a clue. She said, "A penny for your thoughts."

He knew that denying that his mind was busy would only get him in trouble, so he asserted, "I've been working in insurance for a year, and I know the money is good, Baby, but I'm not sure I can see myself doing this same thing over and over again. The reality is that I am working at a place where I really don't want to be."

Taking a puff of Foster's maduro, Tiffany concurred, "Baby, you need to do something to make you happy."

Foster looked his wife of 19 years in the face and stated, semi-confidently, "I want to inspire, encourage, and motivate young men to become better—to become more than what they are. I think I want to teach."

She looked him directly in his eyes then looked down at the inch of bright, white ash on the cigar she was pinching between her thumb and forefinger. She looked back up at her husband and responded, "Okay, go ahead and do it. I'm behind you." Tiffany motioned for her husband to pose for a selfie. They held each other close and smiled for the photograph. She has always supported his dreams.

He looked at the image of himself and his wife on her phone and looked around the lounge. He started to feel uncertain; he thought, "Man, I want to be able to help kids, but teaching and education is a lifestyle. Will she *really* be okay with cutting back on *this* lifestyle?" Foster smiled at Tiffany, "Will I?" He took a slow drag of his cigar and got lost in the music.

CHAPTER 8
I Decide What a Black Man is Every Day

Mr. Higgenbottem gathered the clean, unused paper plates and placed them in the large gray tote marked "PTA." On the short wooden bookshelf behind the tote, he noticed a white book with colorful circles on the cover. He had never seen the book before, so he read the title slowly aloud, "*Whistling Vivaldi: How Stereotypes Affect Us and What We Can Do.*"[60]

Mr. Miller looked up from the stack of PTA Meeting Agendas he had collected from the desks that were unoccupied during the meeting. He had just acquired a copy of Claude Steele's book during a districtwide professional development session, so he wasn't surprised that it stood out to Mr. Higgenbottem, and he was happy that someone other than himself found the concept interesting.

Mr. Higgenbottem paused, placed both hands on the long table in front of him, leaned forward and repeated, "*How stereotypes affect us.* You know, in my generation and generations before me, African-American males—there were certain stereotypes that we had. One of those is being uneducated and not getting a college education. And another is, you know, not being a teacher. When I think about it, we didn't have many teachers who looked like us. In my neighborhood school, there was a Black person in the cafeteria, the custodial staff was Black, and then we had 2 Black teachers: one was a teacher assistant, one was an actual teacher—a 4th grade teacher. Wait … there was a kindergarten teacher as well who was Black, too, Ms. Blocker, and that's it. It's disappointing that we didn't have many people to relate to or to look at so we could make something out of ourselves."

Mr. Miller was happy that Mr. Higgenbottem and Mr. Campbell had stayed behind to help him clean the classroom after the last PTA meeting of the school year. Mr. Higgenbottem was a retired teacher and the most active parent in his school's PTA chapter; and Kamau enjoyed the informal, clean-up chats they would often have after meetings ended.

Mr. Miller responded, "Yeah, I definitely noticed that there wasn't a lot of male teachers, and that was definitely something that I thought about when I decided to become a teacher." He placed the agendas in a manilla folder marked PTA Meeting Agendas. He continued, "There's this brother that I am close with. He teaches at a charter school. We swap stories all the time about how important it is for us to have an influence on these kids. We often come to the same conclusion: there's not enough of us out here to make a difference. We can touch a few kids, but more of our kids are still falling through the cracks because they don't have that male influence. But I tell you what: I'm doing everything I can to be present and available for them. One day last summer, we all got boys that didn't have fathers in the household and the men brought their sons, and we took them to a Pittsburgh Pirates baseball game just to have an outing, just to have some fun. Just so these boys can see with their own eyes and experience that they have brothers, fathers, mentors, pastors, teachers that are doing the right thing and that actually care about their well-being. Now, I'm going to take it even further because I'm putting together a boys' and men's group where we do just that. We talk to these boys. We counsel them. We take them on trips. We tell them the value of education. We tell them the value of spirituality. We help them understand that life has a real critical meaning for them, especially in this country. You, being a Black boy and soon to be a Black man, you have to defy all the odds. You should do it with a smile on your face, too, because we don't have to walk around angry and upset that the world wants to disrespect us." Kamau held the folder in his hands for a few seconds, then placed it in the bottom drawer of the tall, black, steel lateral file cabinet behind his desk.

Mr. Higgenbottem agreed with the importance of helping others. He shared, "When I was coming up, it was required for us to understand that Christian service included more than just going to church, more than just receiving the Holy Communion, more than just all this other stuff that the Bible says or that the Catholic Church outlined for us to do. We have to be there for our fellow men."

Kamau nodded his head at Mr. Higgenbottem, looked at his mentee, Mr. Campbell, and continued, "You know, my job is to help youth and adults understand that it's time for them to be who they are. Stop trying to be like everybody else because if God gave us all unique talents and gifts, then he means for us to exercise them. If he wanted robots, he would have made us all look the same. He would have made us all the same sex. He would have made us all wear the same clothes. We would have been like androids. Who wants to be like that?" He shrugged his shoulders and leaned back against his desk. "But I'll tell you what: when I first got here, there was something really disappointing …" Kamau paused, "I encountered mothers of my students who would hit on me … and get upset that I didn't flirt back. I was even approached by one about what some of the parents *perceived* as my sexuality because I didn't take the bait. It makes me laugh now, but it was nauseating when I started teaching here 5 years ago. Because my focus is and always has been on making their children better students and leaders, I just shook it off and kept it pushing. Eventually, their children's progress won out versus a date." Kamau laughed and shook his head.

"It's really interesting that you would say that," entered David into the conversation, "because we *just* discussed that exact issue in my Student Teaching Seminar the other day." David Campbell was a student teacher from the University of Pittsburgh conducting his clinical internship under the tutelage of Mr. Kamau Miller. David was thrilled to be able to apprentice under another Black man and embraced every opportunity to share space and conversation with him. David shared, "The social construction of homophobia acts as a ritualized mechanism of social control, especially since it has been conveniently (and erroneously) conflated with pedophilia."[61]

Putting the pens he had collected from the desks into the blue plastic bin on Mr. Miller's desk, Mr. Higgenbottom interrupted, "Slow down, slow down, young blood. Say that for me in English." Mr. Miller and Mr. Higgenbottom laughed. Mr. Higgenbottom liked to tease David whenever he felt he was being too "academic."

"My bad, Mr. Higgenbottom," David said smiling. "I'm just talking about this book we're reading called *Real Men or Real Teachers?* by Dr. Paul Sargent. He interviewed men teachers, and one of them said that he was shocked by the parents' approach. He said that they immediately think that he was gay, and they look at him and act like they don't want a gay man teaching their children. Another guy in the book shared that some parents will even be point blank and say to him, 'Why are you teaching here? Don't you think you should be doing xyz? You're very strange to teach'."[62]

Mr. Higgenbottom raised his eyebrows, and Mr. Miller shook his head, "Yeah. The stereotypes are rampant."

Mr. Miller continued, "Another stereotype that I have come across is the *laziness* tag. My coworkers are so astonished at how much time and effort I put into teaching. I spend my weekends going to support my students in their extra-curricular activities, calling parents to let them know how their students are doing—positive and negative. I am the first to arrive and one of the last to leave. Sometimes, I'm here till 8 or 9 o'clock at night. I could be grading papers, tutoring, doing just extra stuff to not only make my days easier but also to help them when they're struggling with things as well. It's not just for my kids either. A lot of my coworkers need help—something going on with their smart board, something with their computer. Today I had to lock my door while we were setting up for the PTA meeting because if I don't, they'll be like, *Hey, I need your help with something*, so my door was locked. Then, I just wave at them from my door to let them know I'll get back with them later. They also find it unusual that I go to students' houses. Many have never seen a Black man in a women's profession who is passionate about teaching. *Now*, most of what I hear from parents is *thank you*. There are some of my co-workers on the other hand," he shook his head and lowered his voice, "I can never do go enough for them." He turned away from the other two men and started erasing the meeting agenda from the dry erase board.

Mr. Higgenbottem understood Mr. Miller's conundrum. But he is an old-school, retired Catholic school teacher, who still held onto some very old-school views. He added, "They call it a women's profession, but before I retired, the most challenging thing for me was having to follow administrators that don't have a clue about how to impact the lives of our boys. The academy at which I taught had all women in the administration. This is not to say that all women do not have a clue because I have seen some phenomenal teachers and principals who could reach our boys. I am saying that *these* women were out of touch."

Mr. Miller stopped erasing the board, squinted, and turned to face Mr. Higgenbottem so that he could hear him more clearly.

Mr. Higgenbottem winked at Mr. Miller and continued, "Thank God that the academy where I taught was connected to the church because at least they could see some of the male leaders and ministers and accountants and people who work for the church administration. In the school, our whole administrative staff in the academy was all women. When I voiced that, when I said something, when I tried to crack the ceiling and get into administration, I was treated like I was saying bad words, I wasn't doing the correct thing, or I was telling people something that was improper. The last time I checked, that was a Biblical-based church and school, where it was clear … and I've heard the Priest preach it: that the man is the head of the household just as Jesus was the head of the church. Men are put in place to lead the family, to guide the church. It does not say women cannot have leadership roles, but when you have a structure set in place where all of your leadership staff are women, what kind of message does that send? Especially if you're in education, and you want boys to see that they can be better than what they see on television, that they can be better than what some of their fathers are or their uncles or whatever, and they can't see that positive influence. How sad is it that they would see me and say, 'Wow, that's *one*. Respect Mr. Higgenbottem'. He's the *only* one." David was fascinated by this deep conversation. He added, "Mr. Higgenbottem, because gender roles were less blatantly unequal within the black community than in the white community, it has been easier for Black women teachers to assume positions of leadership. They could not be preachers in the mainstream churches, but the position of teacher ran a close second in terms of prestige and influence."

Mr. Higgenbottem looked at David intently. He crossed his left arm across his chest and tapped his chin with his right index finger. He asserted, "Uhm … no offense to women, but you're talking about women, and women have women ways and women tendencies. And there are some things that women are going to cloud education with just by the mere fact of their design as being women. Men are about solutions and getting the job done: period, point blank. Women have emotions, and emotion ties up the business of education: point blank, period. And if it's a woman's job, and women do it all the time, and women are in front of the kids, what you expect your kid to turn out like if they're around nothing but women? So they gotta have a male balance: period."

David frowned. He did not agree with his student's father, but he dare not respond disrespectfully. Instead, he walked over to the refreshments table, opened one of the leftover bags of pretzels, popped a pretzel in his mouth, and looked at his mentor, Mr. Miller, for guidance.

Mr. Miller, seeing Mr. Campbell's concern, nodded at his mentee, and attempted to shift the conversation, "There's a huge shortage in male teachers, especially African-American male teachers, so I think also being an educator, part of my role is to show, you know, my colleagues that an African-American male teacher does have a right and can educate students along with Caucasian men or Caucasian women and even African-American women. Also, my role is to help other African-American boys and men see that there's a future in education because I know when I was growing up, becoming a teacher was not a sought after career or profession. Sometimes, it can be difficult for an African-American man to enter the education field," he pointed his hand at Mr. Campbell, who was finishing his small bag of pretzels, and finished, "especially to elementary or early childhood grades, and I think part of it is because there haven't been enough African-American men to do it, you know, to show that we belong here."

David threw his empty pretzel bag in the trash can. He inserted, "During one of my early field experiences, I went over to another elementary school. I was there just to observe for a week. They were actually doing a book study about how to motivate the young African-American males, and that's when the light started coming on. Our boys: they aren't doing good. It's not just enough for me to be there for them. I gotta inspire them even more to do more with their lives—not just be an example but inspire them to do more than what I've done." Mr. Campbell looked at himself in the small mirror on the side of Mr. Miller's file cabinet, straightened his tie, took a deep breath, and continued, "I mean as long as I have breath in my body, as long as I'm in the school system, I'm gonna try my best to make sure that these young Black boys don't become a statistic. That's my biggest driving force. I mean I even sit down with the kids at lunch and ask them, 'You know what they say about you? They say that if you're not proficient by 3rd grade, that … you're gonna probably be in jail, so they're preparing jailhouses for you. Don't be the statistic'. You know what I'm saying? Then, like I said, reading, talking with my professors, and going to professional development, I keep hearing that less than 2 percent of teachers are African-American males. I want to change that statistic, you know what I'm saying? I'm like, I'm trying to rob other majors by telling all my friends to try education." He laughs. "You know, like 50 tried to rob the industry!"[63] Mr. Campbell and Mr. Miller both started dancing and rapping the chorus to the song, "This ain't serious. Being broke can make you delirious!"[64] They slapped hands and laughed. Mr. Campbell continued, "For real! I'm like, Yo man, 'come over here and join me'. You know stuff like that because our young men need it. They really need it."

Mr. Miller agreed with his intern. He was proud of him, his growth, and his passion for teaching. Kamau concurred, "The more African-American men we get in school, the less we have them on the streets. One of the biggest things that I dislike is that people come across a young Black male and they automatically think, 'Uneducated, ain't about nothing, don't know how to talk, all they talk is slang. Oh, what is he up to now?' Just imagine if we actually shine a good light on African-American males and give them an opportunity to actually do something with their life, instead of trying to lock them up all the time. It's kind of like—we can't have blinders on like we don't know what's going on in the world. Even though we're trying to train them up, we still have to address the things that are going on in the world. Because if we don't, then it's like we're just putting a Band-Aid on an entirely serious problem that our youth these days are facing."

David nodded vigorously, "Yeah. That's why my professor calls it the *opportunity* gap rather than the *achievement* gap." He was enjoying his student teaching internship more and more each day. He got excited when he could make connections to what he was learning in his classes.

Mr. Higgenbottem inserted, "Unfortunately, the motives and actions of some men in education have created a microscope on all of us. Sometimes, I felt like I was fighting a battle within the profession as well as this battle as a Black man. On both ends, we have actions of men crippling the power of men. It's amazing how we have the stereotypes of Black men who are trying to make a positive change and then we have the stereotype of Black men that people created by the circulation of Black men occupying prisons, those who are athletes, so forth and so on."

Mr. Miller interjected, "Mr. Higgenbottem, regardless of what a brotha does, they will have something to say, so my philosophy is do all the good you can, include as many as you can, and in the end reinvent instead of reinforcing the negative stereotypes of the Black man. *I decide what a Black man is every day, and no one has to like it.*"

Mr. Campbell stood up and slow clapped. He looked at Mr. Miller and smiled.

Mr. Miller smiled and continued, "I used to wear suits every day: a tie, a shirt, coat. I remember the kids would laugh. When I first started here, the teachers would ask me, 'Where you going? To church?' They called me Preacher Man. I did that for two years. I was teaching third grade, so a lot of times I would be out in the playground playing with the kids with a tie and shirt on. To me, that was setting the tone for the rest of my career, basically. I wanted the kids to understand that I was serious about school and the people that I was working with. I wanted them to understand that I was serious about my profession because I feel like you have to be twice as good as everybody else. I truly believe that. When I had my first open house, I remember all the kids' parents came to see who was teaching their kid. I remember them coming just to see the Black guy that's teaching their kids, which was interesting because that was my first time experiencing something like that. It didn't catch me off guard but … that's why I wore suits and stuff. That first impression they got was a good impression. I just remember them all coming to see. They were all in the hall and even had parents coming that didn't have kids in my class coming to see and meet me." Mr. Miller shook his head. He wasn't smiling anymore. "It was like a never-ending circus. You have to keep proving yourself each year. This is my 5th year, and I'm still proving myself. It's almost like no matter what you do, you still got to do better than what you did last year."

"Let me tell you a story," Mr. Higgenbottem sat down on a student desk, "This was something that I reflected on maybe 12–13 years ago when I was at a crossroads and God brought me into the realm of education. After college, all my jobs were pretty much medical-based. I worked for a medical supply company; then, I worked for a dental insurance company. Then, I worked for a life insurance company. Then, I worked in nursing after that in hospitals and doctor's offices. What took its course there is … I was working on the oncology/hematology floor at Smithtown Hospital Center.[65] That floor is literally … you see more death than anything because these are cancer patients, as well as people with HIV/AIDS, and things like that. You see more people pass than you see recover. That was really depressing for me. I worked overnight, so when I would come in, I would see my patients, make sure they were comfortable, see what they needed. This was all before I even put my bags down. Then, when I went to the locker room to put my stuff away and came back, it was like I had already did a half an hour's worth of work because I cared that much for my patients."

David sat down at a student desk. He did not know that Mr. Higgenbottem had a career in the medical field before he became a teacher, so he was all ears as the older gentlemen shared.

"When I got to work, if I'm walking past their doors to go to the locker room, then I'm stopping before I go just to see that they're okay, and they know I'm on shift that night. But …," Mr. Higgenbottem held up his right hand with a pointed index finger, "when I started making these relationships, I started getting flack from other nurses—because it was a lot of jealousy, too—if I had a bond with somebody that they didn't have.

It was just a whole lot of jealousy up there. It was like, *Higgenbottem's spending too much time with this patient. He spends too much time with that one.* It started to become a real headache with that aspect of it. Long story short, I had gotten close with this lady that was an HIV patient. She was real cool and everything. When she passed, it was like … I had known her maybe for 4 or 5 months because she would come in and out for her treatments or whatever. That last time, it was just like I kind of felt in my spirit that that was the last time I was going to see her. Then, she passed, and I was like, 'Wow, can I really do this?' The last straw was when my best friend's aunt, she had cancer and she passed. The night that I came in—I was off the day before …. When I came in that next night and I went to see her before I put my stuff down and she smiled and was like, 'I was waiting for you'. I was like, 'Oh yeah, I'll be right back. I'm just going to put my stuff down'. I hugged her. I said, 'I'm just going to put my stuff down and I'll come talk to you and watch a little TV before I see my other patients'. Not knowing until I came back and she was gone that her saying *I was waiting for you* was really, literally, 'I was waiting for you to get here', before she passed. I took that as her saying *thank you* to me for caring for her while she was in there because when I got back, she was gone. Then, I had to make that phone call to my best friend and her family and let them know that she had passed. That whole night was just hard because I tried to see my other patients but that was my family. Instead, I kind of just stayed down there with her family and consoled them and things like that. In that moment, I was like, 'Wow, I don't know if I can do this anymore'. Because it's one thing to treat people and you send them home, but when people that you treat and you form relationships with, they pass away, that was too hard for me to swallow."

"Wow, Mr. Higgenbottem," Kamau said. "I knew that you had another career before you taught, but I had no idea it was this. From dealing with nonsense with your colleagues to losing those you care about so often, that sounds like it was difficult. Did you ever work with children at the hospital?"

Mr. Higgenbottem shook his head, "No. You know, that whole time, my Alpha brother, Tony, worked right across the way at Children's American Medical Center[66] because it's right across the street from Smithtown

Hospital Center. He's a psychologist. He would tell me how he would get mostly kids, and some that had cancer would pass away. He ended up coming out of there. He moved down to North Carolina and ended up doing psychology with young adults because he couldn't take being in the hospital setting and these kids passing away. I was like, 'Dude, if I know I can't handle the grown people and I love kids like that, I'm not going to be able to stomach the young people passing away like that'. So … just to cut the story down, I ended up coming out of there, and I went to work for Quest[67] doing stuff in the lab, drawing blood, all that kind of stuff. I was like, 'Okay, this is easier, more flexible schedule. I can float around'. Then that got old after a while. I was like, 'Lord, do you really want me to do medicine?' Because around that time I was like, 'I need to go ahead and get my butt into medical school'."

"Medical school?" Mr. Campbell and Mr. Miller asked in unison.

Mr. Higgenbottem laughed, "I didn't go to medical school right away. I did the nursing thing because it was quicker to get in school and do things of that nature and come out. It was cheaper, too. I went into nursing because my children were young. My son, Woody, was born right after I graduated from Morehouse. I already had a daughter who's three years older than him—my oldest daughter. I was like, 'I need to make that money. I need to help bring that bread in for my family'. Then, I was thinking about if I should go back. The Lord kept saying 'No, that's not what I have for you'. Then, I was like all I have to do is take the MCAT again and do my applications. I was about to do it anyway, but God just kept saying, 'No, no, no'. I didn't do it. I ended up quitting my job at Quest because I literally hated it that much. I quit, and I ended up moving back home with my mother for a minute." He paused. The three men were silent for a few seconds. Kamau and David were eager to hear the rest of the story, so they stayed quiet.

"Now, check this out," Higgenbottem continued, "I was already an ordained deacon because I got ordained when I was at Morehouse my freshman year. Then, the Lord started tugging at me that he wanted me to preach and teach his word. I was like 'Huh, what? Now you're messing with me again, Lord? I'm not a preacher'." He laughed, "But then my background as a public speaker—because I did oratorical contests since I was probably early teens—so he was preparing me to publicly speak even way back then. He was like, 'I want you to do this'. And my cousin, who is a pastor of his own church, I spoke to him about it. He was like 'If the Lord is telling you to do it, you need to do it'." He encouraged me to take some classes and read some books. I started doing that, and I think about a year later, I started taking 2 and 3 classes at the seminary, just really embracing it. Then, through various people and different churches, I got opportunities early on to preach, to teach and do youth nights and Sunday school teaching. I got my experience up and then God just kept blessing me and blessing me. Then, lo and behold, a church in my community was opening up a brand new Christian academy. My mother worked with one of the parishioners here. She was like, "They've got a school over there; you need to apply." He threw his silver-haired head back and laughed, "I promise you the first thing that came out of my mouth was 'I'll see them kids after school, help them with their homework, we can even go on little outings and stuff like that, but being in a classroom with a whole bunch of kids?'" He chuckled, "I was like, 'No, Ma'. Then this voice, it was the Lord again, but it was also my conscience, 'You're a grown man, Slim. You need to get back up out your mother's house'. I was like, 'You know what? You're right. I was not raised to be at home'. I sent over my resume—emailed it over. How about they called me the same day! I think I interviewed two days later and got the call the next day to be a teacher there. I was there 12 years before I retired."

Mr. Higgenbottem stretched the palms of his hands out in front of him and looked down at them. "You talk about having to prove yourself over and over again, Mr. Miller," he curled his fingers over to form two tight fists. Then, he opened his hands again, "These hands have provided comfort to families in hard times, held dying patients, prayed for people in need, and written lesson plans. They've done a lot, and what is true throughout all of that is that when people see this Black man's hands, they see me as dangerous." He closed his left eye and looked at the two younger men through his squinted right eye, "You young cats know the song *Fight the Power*?"

Mr. Miller scoffed, "By Public Enemy? Of course I do!"

As if cued by a deejay, the three men all started rapping the same exact verse, "Elvis was a hero to most ..."[68]

Mr. Higgenbottem was pleased that the younger gentlemen knew the song so well. He asserted, "Back in my day, becoming a teacher was a way for us to *fight the powers that be*,[69] a way to react to the social and educational inequities: both, the underlying and prevalent ones that Mr. Campbell, there, mentioned earlier. It was how we committed to social justice and challenged those stereotypes people have of us." He winked at Mr. Campbell.

Mr. Campbell was in awe. Mr. Higgenbottem had taken them on a journey through a long story, during which he wasn't sure where he was going with it at first, but it all made sense now. He sat up tall and leaned forward onto the desk.

Just then, Mr. Higgenbottem's twin sons, Jeff and Greg, walked into the classroom. Even though only Jeff was a student in Mr. Miller's classroom, both boys hugged Mr. Miller and Mr. Campbell before greeting their father.

"You boys finished with piano?," Mr. Higgenbottem asked the boys, dressed in dark blue denim jeans and short-sleeve polo shirts—Jeff's shirt was burgundy, and Greg's was light blue. His sons were taking a piano class after school with the music teacher, Mrs. Cox. The boys really liked Mrs. Cox and so did Mr. Higgenbottem. She reminded him of his second-grade teacher, Miss Page, a teacher who had a great influence on him because he remembered her as a really nice lady. She was also very structured and very nurturing in the classroom. He recalled always having this feeling that he wanted to please her: that was always important to him. At the time, the other kids called him the teacher's pet, but he didn't care. In fact, that was his motive. He wanted to make sure that she was happy with everything that he did that year. She was a very intelligent lady. His parents got along with her. Like Mr. Miller, he had the kind of mother that was always there: PTSA President, going on the field trips, chaperoning, doing this and doing that. Consequently, he learned early on that it was important for him, as a parent, to be involved with his children's education. He learned that from his mother. Being that she interacted with Miss Page very well made a huge difference for him as a student. He was never the type of kid that acted up and all that kind of stuff, so his parents getting to know his teachers was never a big deal for him. As a young kid, since he saw his mom there anyway getting to know his teachers, that became normal to him; that's what parents did, so that's what he did.

Jeff and Greg replied in unison, "Yes Sir."

Mr. Higgenbottem stood in front of his sons, who were standing side-by-side, and held them by their shoulders. His right hand on Greg's left shoulder and his left hand on Jeff's right shoulder, he looked at his sons, "Good. Listen, go wait for me on the bench by the front office while I finish helping Mr. Miller and Mr. Campbell clean up. I love you boys." Mr. Higgenbottem took his hands off the boys' shoulders; they nodded affirmatively, waved to Mr. Miller and Mr. Campbell, and left the classroom to wait for their father as told.

Mr. Higgenbottem looked around to see if anything else needed to be cleaned up before he went home with his children, "Alright, gentlemen, I need to get these boys home. Mr. Miller, you good?"

Mr. Miller smiled and shook Mr. Higgenbottem's hand. "Thanks so much for your help and the conversation … as usual."

Mr. Campbell stood up, walked over to Mr. Higgenbottem, and shook his hand, "Sir, I've learned so much about you today. Thank you for sharing your story. I admire how you show up for us and for your children, here at school. I think it's awesome how much you tell them that you love them. We don't hear that enough."

Mr. Higgenbottem held onto Mr. Campbell's hand and smiled, "Young man, my commitment is all about them because they need to understand that they have a father that loves them. They have a father that wants them here. They have a father that wants to be around them, a father that wants to talk to them, a father that wants to educate them, a father that wants to guide them. A lot of kids don't have that. Then, the kids that have fathers in the home, but they still don't know that their father loves them and things like that. I was a child that grew up and my father never said that he loved me. Never. I can probably count on one hand my entire life in which he did say that he loved me. I tell my kids that I love them every day. Because I want them to understand that it is not some bad thing for your father to tell you that he loves you, for your father to hug you, to kiss you, to caress you, and look in your eyes and tell you that he loves you.

Kids don't have that. That's always looked at as a female characteristic. 'I'm going to get that from Mom. Yes, I'm going to have that bond with Mom, but Dad, he's this certain way. I don't know if I can hug him. I don't know if I can talk to him'. I try to get rid of those gray areas—of those lines between me and my children, as well as the kids that I've worked with. Because if any child here at school can come talk to me, then that's a victory, and I praise God for that because that's what I'm here for. I thought that my working with kids would entail me being in medicine still, but he wanted me to do it through education, through the church, and through fatherhood. I embrace it wholeheartedly." Mr. Higgenbottom let go of Mr. Campbell's hand and picked up the black leather portfolio in which he kept his PTA information. He looked back at Mr. Campbell, "In my house, we push God first, making sure they do what they're supposed to do, be respectful, do well with their academics, and love their family. I spend a lot of my time with my boys and pretty much most of the day, I'm here. My wife, she's an accountant, and she does a lot of work during the accounting season, so she's rarely home. That's pretty much my life. My life is being with my boys and being with my family. And that's what being a Black man is to me." He nodded to the two teachers, "Good day, gentlemen. Don't stay here too late." Mr. Higgenbottom waved and turned to walk out the room.

Mr. Campbell waved to Mr. Higgenbottom as he left the classroom and walked over to the small desk that he had arranged for himself in the back of the room. He moved three pencils from the left of his desk to the right. He looked out the window. He was grateful that Mr. Higgenbottom had peeled back some of his layers today. David understood him a bit more now than he did yesterday.

Mr. Miller looked up from his desk. He had sat down at his desk and was organizing a pile of graphic organizers to distribute during the next day's reading lesson. "You aight over there?" he asked Mr. Campbell.

Mr. Campbell was deep in thought, "Listening to Mr. Higgenbottom today has me thinking." He paused, "Can I share something personal with you?"

"Of course. What you say here is between me and you, Bruh," Kamau assured David.

David tried to smile, but his mind was 100 miles away. He opened up, "When I was growing up, I had to raise my younger siblings. I was born to 2 parents who were steadily in the use of drugs. I have three younger sisters and a younger brother as well. My brother is 5 years younger than I am. I have kinda been in the poverty line all my life." He paused and took a deep breath, "I grew up going to 5 different elementary schools because we moved around so much. When my parents got divorced at 10, it was like I was thrust into a position that I didn't ask for. At 10, you want to be a kid, but I was thrust into the responsibility of caring for my younger sisters because my mother moved out and took my brother with her, and my dad worked in the evening. In the evening time, I'm this 10-year-old kid looking after my younger sisters. That whole time, from probably 10 to about 16 years old, that was my primary responsibility—helping to raise them. I finally got a little stabilized when we lived with our grandmother until I graduated high school. At that point, my family structure was breaking down again. My mom, she was moving from home to home, and it got so I kinda had to mediate where my younger brother was going and kind of follow up with him. What I would do—my goal was … I was getting ready to graduate high school, so my goal was to go to school. I was so confused and unaware." He shook his head. "I assumed that by looking at the college dormitory set-up … so they all have suites, and I thought that we were going to be living in an apartment. So I told him, 'Look man, I'll just move you in with me, and I'll enroll you at school'. Well, I found out very quickly that that wasn't the case; it wasn't gonna work out like that. To this day, me and my mom don't have the greatest relationship."

"Man, I didn't know that. I'm really sorry to hear that," Mr. Miller inserted.

"Yeah. I know. Thanks, Man," Mr. Campbell responded. He continued, "I was thinking about Mr. Higgenbottem's story, how he's helped people, and how he's so present for his children. My life wasn't easy, and I've had to do a lot on my own, so a big thing for me is to be able to repay people for what they've done for me. You know, I just feel like it's so hard to thank some people for what they've done for me. I wish that sometimes I could just give that gift to people because they've given some stuff to me. For them, it probably wasn't much. To them, it was something normal—it wasn't abnormal.

It's like, it's like …," David leaned his head to the right, and his eyes lit up, "*teaching*. You just give them something just because that's the right thing to do. That's what you do. But for me, it was like, teachers have given me half of my world. They always gave me encouragement, and it ain't no way I could pay money for that. They gave me things that transformed me as a person. I can't even … I can't get beyond it. You know what I mean?"

"Yeah, I do." Mr. Miller concurred.

"I know I have to be accountable," David began. "I just remember all of my teachers. I think that was a big part of me becoming a teacher because they all had an effect on my life one way or another, good or bad. And I just want people to see that all Black men aren't trifling, disrespectful, only worried about what they can get from women, only trying to get over doing the wrong thing, drinking, drugs, in jail. Kids need to see *us*." Mr. Campbell moved his right hand in a circular motion, indicating that he was talking about himself, Mr. Miller, and Mr. Higgenbottem. He looked down at his hands.

Mr. Miller felt Mr. Campbell's words down to his core. He felt them as if he had spoken them himself. He believed them. He walked over to Mr. Campbell, who had a discouraged look on his face, put his hand on Mr. Campbell's right shoulder and asked, "Can I share something with you?"

"Most certainly," Mr. Campbell responded.

"My first student teaching internship, I didn't pass," Mr. Miller shared.

Mr. Campbell looked up from his hands shocked.

Mr. Miller continued, "and I thought it was very interesting—the interaction I had at the school because it was like the first time I was working at a school that was predominantly Caucasian people. And uhm … the teacher that I was working with, she was a younger Caucasian teacher There were many times that we had conversations. She would say things like 'Oh yeah, you can do that Mr. Miller' and 'Oh yeah, you can just take this'. But she was setting me up for the okie doke, pretty much. She was giving me suggestions of things that she did and things like that, and then she would come back around to my professor and tell her I wasn't prepared and that I was doing things illegally when she was the one who recommended that I do those things, you know? For example, there was one time, I was using my cell phone on the playground. She went back and told my professor that I was using my cell phone, but at the same time, she using hers, and there was no problem with that at all. At the time, I wasn't familiar with FERPA, or taking pictures of students and stuff like that, but I wasn't taking pictures of students. It was the fact that I had a cellular device out, and I wasn't monitoring the students like I should have been, uhm, they kinda sorta stuck me kinda hard on that. But uhm, that was a learning experience because it showed me that even today … how race and how different perspectives can affect a person—in particular, in this case, it was me. Thinking about the young, African-American children that were in that school. The majority of the school was young Caucasian individuals, and the demographics in this class was predominantly Caucasian with maybe 1 or 2 Black kids. I could just notice that those kids were lagging behind, and it wasn't necessarily because they didn't have the ability to do the work. It was because the attention wasn't paid to them and stuff like that. So that motivated me to go on a little bit more. Even though I didn't like it at first, you know, having to repeat my internship and all that good stuff, after I sat down and thought about it for a little while, I saw that it was necessary for me to see different viewpoints and see different things that's going on in the school system. Many of my parents are too engaged with their own lives to even notice that their kid could be further along if they gave them the proper amount of attention in helping them learn. This goes for my more advanced students as well as the ones who are behind. But if someone spoke of *my* legacy, who I am, I want them to know that I put *everything* I could into trying to make every kid, every house, every street a little bit better through what I do."

Mr. Campbell looked at his mentor and smiled. He shook his head in agreement and felt grateful for the day. The PTA meeting went great. The school year was finishing strong, and he was blessed to be able to engage older Black men in conversation about teaching. Yet, he worried about the Black boys in his school. He worried about his peers whose internships were not as empowering as his. He worried about the Black male teachers around the country who have to shuck and jive just to be seen and appreciated for the important work they do. He was worried … so he decided, in that moment, to let that worry fuel him. He knew that there was so much work to be done, and he was happy to have Mr. Miller by his side to do it.

CHAPTER 9
The Solution Has to Be a Collective Effort

"THREE hours?!" Kamau looked up at the flight departure board and then down at his watch. "What am I going to do for 3 hours in this airport?" Kamau looked around Concourse D of the Hartsfield–Jackson Atlanta International Airport, spotted Ludacris' new restaurant about 20 feet away, and rubbed his hands together. "Chicken + Beer it is!" he said aloud. Kamau grabbed the handle on his black wheeled carry-on bag and started walking toward the eatery. He was not happy about the 3-hour layover ahead of him, but he was looking forward to his destination: The Windy City itself—Chicago, IL. He'd never been to The Chi, and though he wasn't heading on a vacation, he always enjoyed engaging other educators and folk interested in improving the conditions of Black and Brown children. And the Critical Race Studies in Education Association conference was just that place for him.

The conference started on Thursday, so he had to get a substitute to cover his class. He hated leaving his students under someone else's supervision for two whole days. He loved and understood their quirks and silly ways, but not everyone did, so he hoped they were behaving themselves with the sub.[70] He had conversed with his students before dismissal this afternoon. He told them all about the conference: how he would be meeting other educators and sharing how he uses HipHop to help them learn. They promised to be good while he was gone. Remembering their promise brought him solace; he always wanted to be a positive influence on his students, so their faith and excitement was meaningful to him. Lost in thought about his children in Pittsburgh and not fully paying attention to his surroundings, Kamau bumped shoulders with another Black man who had stopped in the middle of the walkway to check his work emails on his phone. "My bad, Bro. Excuse me," Kamau stopped to apologize.

The gentleman looked up from his phone as if he didn't even feel the shoulder bump, "Huh? Oh, you're good, Bro."

The two men were about to continue their separate ways when they simultaneously noticed something familiar about one another. "Profound Gentlemen?" They both asked and then laughed and nodded their heads. They gave one another dap and introduced themselves.

"I'm Shaka. Shaka Barnett," the gentleman offered, "from North Carolina."

"Kamau Miller. Harlem, New York." Kamau responded. "Nice button." He referred to a small black and red button on the left lapel of Shaka's tweed blazer. The round button read "PG" in red font inside the red outline of an apple with a black background. Kamau recognized the logo of Profound Gentlemen, an organization that supports Black and Brown male educators.

Shaka nodded, "Nice shirt." He motioned to the black tee shirt Kamau was wearing. The words Profound Gentleman were inscribed in large red capital letters to the left of the same apple outline on Shaka's button. Kamau looked down at his shirt and smiled. Shaka inquired, "It's not often I run into other Black male educators. Where do you teach?"

Kamau agreed. In his travels, he often meets other brothers, but this is the first time he's found himself inadvertently in space with another Black male teacher. "The Hill District in Pittsburgh, PA. Third grade," Kamau responded, "You?"

"Greensboro, North Carolina. Fifth grade for the past 4 years," Shaka replied, "but I've taught PreK, first, second, and fourth grades as well."

"Wow, PreK? First? You've rumbled with the little ones! That's what's up!" Kamau was pleasantly surprised to also meet a Black man who has worked with young children because all his experience has been in the upper grades.

"Yeah," Shaka shared, "My first teaching job, I actually interviewed for second grade, but they switched at the last minute and put me with first grade because the second grade, at the time, was the highest class that we had. It was a new school. We had PreK through second. Now we're all the way up to eighth grade. We actually just graduated our first eighth grade class on Friday, this past Friday." Just then, Shaka's phone beeped. He shook his head as he looked at the flight delay alert on his phone and said, "Man. My flight is delayed until 8:06." It was a quarter to six.

Kamau shook his head, "Congratulations on the graduation. But yeah, Man. These airports are something. I'm here on a 3-hour layover."

"Man." Shaka, always up for good conversation with a fellow educator, motioned to the restaurant they had been standing in front of, "Let's grab a brew."

"Word." Kamau responded walking toward Chicken + Beer.

The two elementary school educators located a pair of seats at the bar and settled themselves. After the bartender took their drink orders, Kamau thought about his new comrade as a primary grades teacher and asked, "So what you think about what some people say about men who teach young children? What's your motivation?"

Shaka laughed and shook his head, "My motivation? Hmpf. I do it for the kids. I left a job where I was making more money, so, you know, if money was my motivation, I would not be sitting here. I guess it's like I just do me, so I'm not too concerned about perceptions or anything like that. I've seen the tide turning a lot more recently—more Black men and young Black men in teaching in general. But ... those who know me know that I am very secure in whatever it is that I'm doing. I just see more rewards in this profession than in most other professions. I'm here to serve children."[71]

Kamau reasserted, "I feel you on that. Many of the brothers who I grew up with who are just like me—very ambitious, very dedicated, determined—are lawyers, politicians, doctors, whatever. They don't necessarily get on the elementary school track because they're not earning the kind of money they need to support their families. So sometimes they do other things strictly because of financial reasons. You ever think about teaching bigger kids, like middle school?"

"Certainly. I was in finance, and my thing was math. But in NC, in order to teach middle school math, I had to take 18 hours of math and 18 hours of another subject, and I would've had to be in school for an additional two years to meet those requirements because I didn't have them already. My advisor told me if I did elementary ed, that I could go through the same plan of study I was on and graduate on time. Then, just take the Praxis for middle and the Praxis for high school after I graduated. So I was like, 'Well cool, and that was my plan. But I haven't been able to leave the little ones'." Shaka shrugged his shoulders.

"I get it. I totally do," Kamau began as he was interrupted by his phone ringing. Melle Mel's voice pierced the low hum of conversation that filled the bar, *Don't push me 'cause I'm close to the edge.*[72]

"The Message," Shaka nodded to the beat while looking down at the menu, "Great choice of ringtone."

Kamau sending the call to voicemail, concurred, "Thanks, Man. I'm a HipHop head." The bartender placed two beers on the bar in front of the gentlemen. Kamau had ordered an IPA.[73] He smiled at her, "Thank you."

Shaka nodded at the bartender, "Thank you, Nia." He had read her name tag when they first ordered, and he found it important to address people by their names whenever possible. "HipHop head. For sure. Me, too, Kamau," Shaka responding to Kamau's last thought. He held his Stella Artois up to Kamau before taking a sip, "well … at least the good stuff." He glanced down at his beer. "The evolution of HipHop is just not appealing to me these days. My generation was more real. I really dislike much of what the students listen to these days. I just can't stomach it. I go back and download a lot of old school stuff and have that stuff on heavy rotation. I also like gospel HipHop artists like LeCrae."

Remembering the young woman's mention of Canton Jones at the pre-Kwanzaa celebration he had attended with Diane 6 months ago, Kamau said, "Yeah, there are some really hot gospel HipHop artists out today."

Shaka asserted, "Fact. Their stuff has the same style that my students listen to sometimes but very different lyrics. I am just opposed to most of the new stuff because of the messages that are behind the lyrics, the videos and the lifestyle that's portrayed within the African-American community. It leaves me preaching to the kids more because they are being led astray. The lyrics and the images of today are disheartening. The fact that BET and MTV and all these other streaming sites keep on repeating the same thing over and over—even the radio stations repeating the same message over and over and over again. Basically, the message is not positive for our future, not positive for African-American people. The image they show the kids is a negative image, you know?"

"I hear you on that," Kamau started, "men of our generation are more conscious! We had more positive and politically-laced rap back in the day. We were about movements, history, and civil rights. We are fighters but not quick to pick up a gun or turn to drugs to solve our problems. We are lovers of our women. Not prone to disrespect them or use them as objects of our desires."

Shaka looked at Kamau, "Exactly. Growing up being a Catholic boy, strong parental unit, we believed in family, believed that everyone has their own role in the family, and we all have to contribute. I worked in summer programs, and that put me in a role of working as a community partner, working as an assistant, supporting a greater vision. I always seemed to be in an environment where if it wasn't family, it was programs and initiatives where I still had something to contribute, and what I had to contribute was important to the positive success of the overall program … or … you know, family. The HipHop genre today: the things that they're saying, not a lot of that music is positive, not a lot of it is inspirational. So, for a long time, I didn't like it for that very reason. *Ya'll not putting on a good message for us. Ya'll not giving our kids a positive image to follow out there. You giving them an image that being a drug dealer is good, fine and dandy.* I mean, I've been doing some research. There was some good behind some of these songs, but at the same time, it was very few and far between that I found a good HipHop song that had a good, clean message. You know, and it's like I said, a lot of the stuff that I hear on the radio nowadays is like talking about sex, money, and murder. And our kids, they sing this stuff, come in the classroom saying 'You ratchet!' and stuff like that, and I'm like, 'What is ratchet?'" He laughed at himself.

Kamau laughed as well, "One of the things that makes this generation of Black men teachers unique is that we are old enough but yet young enough to understand HipHop and how we can use it to relate fully with the generation of kids that we teach. That's one of the things that I find in the African-American community; music is a big thing for us, but we gotta use it the correct way."

Shaka took a sip of his beer and placed the bottle down on the bar. He responded, "Hmpf. I definitely work hard to relate to my students. We all relate to music because it speaks about life, and HipHop, in general, speaks about life and the struggle. But we …" Shaka pointed to himself and Kamau, "… used our music to bond, as opposed to today, where it seems like music is mostly divisive; the things that are being said in the music, the images that are being portrayed. We had songs like *Self-Destruction* and artists like KRS-One, Heavy D, Queen Latifah, and people like that, who were giving positive images of what rap was. Public Enemy, militancy—things like that. It just isn't as positive as it used to be, so it's not as useful lyrically as it was in the 90's. I have shared with the kids about how the *positive* rap artists aren't as popular as the average rap star. I've also challenged them to actually listen to some artists who don't have to be censored. Nowadays everything is about sex, sex, sex, drugs, drugs, drugs, drinking, drinking, drinking, cars, cars, cars and clothes, clothes, clothes. I have a hard time relating to that." Shaka took a breath, looked down the bar, and signaled Nia. "Nia, how are the wings? Any good?"

She wiped her hands with a small white towel. "They're pretty good. Popular. I like them," Nia replied.

"Nice. Give me the hot wings and fried cheese sticks, please. Thank you so much." Shaka said.

As Shaka ordered his food, Kamau was thinking about Shaka's last statement and reviewing the menu simultaneously. He didn't quite consider HipHop to have such a deleterious effect; however, he agreed that the music has severely changed over the years. Most importantly, he was grateful that he did not have to spend his 3-hour layover sitting and scrolling social media. He was also hungry—for food and more conversation. Kamau thought about where and when he first started to understand the importance of relating to students. He remembered a teacher he had in the ninth grade named Mrs. Charley. She was this really funny, no-nonsense lady with silvery gray hair and dark skin. She didn't play, but she had the best personality you could ever ask for in a teacher. She had a great relationship with his mother, and she treated him like he was a good kid, a real star student. Years later, after he graduated from high school, he would still go back to the school to see her, just to continue his relationship with her. She was a phenomenal teacher, somebody that any child that was aspiring to a career in education would look up to and kind of model after. He hadn't realized it then, but he did now.

Kamau shared, "When I think about relating to kids, I think about my 9th grade teacher. She's the first teacher who I feel really tried to relate to me—to us. I was just thinking about her, and I've realized that some of my policies and mannerisms come directly from the way she used to run our classroom. She always made sure you understood every rule that she had. She rarely repeated herself more than once. If she wanted something done, you know it was to be done. If you had any issues with it she always invited you to go tell the principal and sit in the office if you didn't like something." The men laughed. Kamau continued, "I'm the same way, but I also have that balance of that personality where the kids know that I can joke, I can play, I can laugh with them. I can be laid back, but when they know there's a test coming up or a quiz coming up, or there are things that need immediate focus and attention, then that's what we're going to jump on. When we have days where we might have a lab that's not so involved that they can get into it and have some fun, then they also understand that as well."

"That's what's up," Shaka interjected.

"Yeah," Kamau agreed. "She would always explain things fully. Like I know some people in general and some teachers as well, they'll give instructions from a book and be like, 'Okay, get to work'. But she was always one to take it a step further, 'Okay the book says this', and then she'll give it another way, give examples, and then say, 'Okay, if you have any questions. And if that's still not clear, then let me know'. It's always that she would go that extra mile for any of her students. That always stood out to me, and I've always tried to be like that, you feel me? One students could feel good around. HipHop helps me create that kind of space."

"I feel you, Bruh." Shaka continued, "So … when I was in the 11th grade, I had a white teacher named Michael O'Shea. He's probably the only …

I won't say the only, hmm ... but to this point, he is the only white man that I've ever loved and respected like he was one of my parents or something, like he was family. He instilled something in me that nobody else did. He was a no-nonsense person. He pretty much told all of us that since we were in a Catholic school that cost thousands of dollars to be in, that we were obviously privileged to be here. He said, 'You need to understand that your education comes with a higher price'. And I've always kept his directive at heart. I decided early on that I wanted to uplift others. And I started to write music. In fact, I did a song with one of my fellow Call Me Mister brothers. We actually did some educational HipHop for students, but ... I think I was really into meaning, flow, and preciseness .... There's just something about using language in a creative way .... And one of the things I hate about HipHop now is that people just rap stuff that doesn't make sense. You know, at least in older rap music, you can understand some people's struggle. You can understand what they were going through. You can understand ... it's almost uplifting. Even though it could be derogatory sometimes, it still had some uplifting components to it."

Kamau asserted, "The problem is much bigger than HipHop alone though. Black culture, not just HipHop culture, has always taught young Black men that you have to be tough. HipHop culture just sensationalizes that ideology."

Nia interrupted, "Excuse me, gentlemen." She looked at Kamau, "Can I get you anything from the menu?"

Kamau looked down at the menu and replied, "Yeah. Can I have the burger, as is, and onion rings please?" He looked at Shaka's nearly empty bottle, "and another round of beers."

Shaka pointed at Kamau. Nia nodded her head. "Thanks," Kamau said.

As Nia walked away, Shaka started, "Black men from the HipHop Generation stood for something greater than themselves—community, love for their people, justice, freedom, stability. Where's the substance in the HipHop today? I want to be able to listen something. I want to be able to put in Nas and Biggie or Jay-Z and hear their message in their music because they're telling you a story. They're giving you glimpses of their life but also telling a story at the same time. Guess what? It sounds good, and it's over a nice beat. For me, I'm not the kind where I'm like, 'Oh man, that joint is banging', and you're just listening to the beat. If I'm not feelin your words, I can't listen to you. Because you can have the best beat in the world. You can be Lil Wayne, some of his beats are great, but I want to hear what you got to say. Therefore, I'm not buying your music. I'm not promoting your music. I don't like you, pretty much. It has to be something that's feeding me. Here's another example: I can't really relate to all the weed smoking, all that kind of stuff, but man, Dre laying those beats down, the whole time, I'm also like, 'You know what? I know who I am. They make it sound good, but no weed's going to touch my lips. They make it sound great, but I'm not jumping in bed with nobody. They make it sound great, but I'm not dropping out of school and saying I'm going to be an artist and just forget education. I'm not going to sell drugs on the corner'. And that fortitude came from it being instilled in me at a younger age that I have my own mind and that I can think for myself and make my own decisions. See, the thing that a lot of people don't understand is that what you listen to feeds into your psyche. It feeds into your spirit. It feeds into your inner man. If you're constantly putting that stuff in your hearing, then it messes with your mental state and you start to believe it. If you tell all the girls that's they're B's and hoes, guess what? That's what they're going to grow up thinking they are. Some of the little girls now who walk around here shaking their tails and don't know why they're doing it because they saw it on a video and they think it's cute, then to see some parent saying that they're cute and cheering them on and stuff like that, look at what you're doing to your child." Shaka paused to take a breath. He knew that many saw his views as outdated, but he held fast to them. "Our youth see HipHop figures as role models; they see these *role models* and see quick money and fame. Rappers rarely have positive songs and lyrics, so HipHop leads young men astray. If more of us don't step up, we are going to lose a lot more kids to the stereotypes and self-destructive images. I think the solution has to be a collective effort between parents, schools, churches, and media."

"Oh, it definitely has to be a collective effort!" Kamau sat up straight on the stool as Nia brought out their second round of beers. He checked the time on the wall behind her. It was 6:38 p.m. "but … I think that we spend too much time trying to make our youth into what we want them to be and not what they want to be and what they are good at. Think about it this way: When HipHop was first born, they were like, 'This is a bad thing. It won't last more than a couple of years and then it will fade out.' At first, pretty much the rest of the music world ignored it, but look at it today. You can't find one music label that doesn't have a few rap artists on it because they know that it's going to sell. It's a billion-dollar business because if you look at it, the White suburban kids are the ones that buy most of the music. Once they saw that, that's when they knew that they needed to get into it because that's where their money was going to come from. I bring in album sales or concert tickets and have discussions with my students about the financial aspects of the industry. I try to infuse it as much as I can because that's what they listen to, so they're always in awe or just happy that someone older than them listens or even knows about the same things that interests them. I use slang, hip sayings, and figurative language to get points across in science. I use imagery to connect urban life, suburban life, and education to help my students to express themselves in ways and terms that are beneficial to them." Kamau sipped his beer. "Just the way I talk. I don't talk like uhm … *a White guy would*. I talk like I always talk. I don't switch that up. I talk to the kids the way they're used to—the way their parents talk. I just don't use any profanity. The way I dress, the word problems that I create in math: it's not *Sally bought some new drapes for her home*. It's *Tomika wanted money for some new Jays*, you know? Things like that, and the kids—it makes them wanna work the problems out. I use their names—Mikhail, Tomika—in the problems, like *Tomika needed $250 to get the new LeBron James Elites*. I used Tomika's name because she likes those shoes. So the new ones are two-fifty. I was like, *Well, she needs two-fifty. She has ¾ of the money. How much more money does she need?* They're like, 'Oh. I've seen those shoes. They do cost $250. So if you got ¾ of it….'"

Nia placed Shaka's food in front of him and told Kamau that his would be out soon. Kamau smiled and continued, "They know *of* means multiply in a word problem, so I give them a calculator, and they work it out to figure out how much they had and subtract to see how much they need. It is always a big success using stuff like that—just using the terminology that they're used to. I'm just using HipHop to better relate to students. If my lesson has even just a name they've heard of, they're ten times more interested in the material I'm presenting."

Taking a pause from his wings, Shaka looked at Kamau. He didn't completely disagree with his new colleague, "I do think it's important, not just for male teachers but all teachers, to understand their kids, have some connection. I have kids at my school who are just straight nerdy, just straight A's and don't do anything else. I'm like, 'You have to be well rounded'. Being book smart is great, but if you're so up here." Shaka held his hand up above his head to mark a high level, "that people can't relate to you, what is your quality of life really going to be? Are you going to be some CEO sitting in an office giving commands, but you really don't have anybody that can relate to you? Or are you going to be a person that people admire, honor, love and respect that they know that they can come to you. You can still be that CEO, you can still be that person that's at the top of anything, but you want to make sure that you have the skills to socially and spiritually connect with people, too. That's what life is. If you don't know anything about the culture or have an idea about what kind of music or what kind of movies or what kind of TV shows they're looking at, then I don't see how you can relate to them. We have to know what's going on within our culture." He bit one of his cheese sticks, chewed for a few seconds, and paused. "In fifth grade, we got the big science assessment. Talk some more about how you integrate HipHop and science."

"Thank you," Kamau said to Nia as she placed his food in front of him. He responded, "I use YouTube Science Raps. I talk to my kids about how a rapper or singer might put together a song. I get them to think about how Tupac wrote a poetry book, *The Rose That Grew from Concrete*.[74] I use it in my poetry units because I think it's quite profound, but I also have students write poetry as it relates to our science unit content. Then, I show them how using the Scientific Method—observation, predicting, and hypothesizing—are key elements that require much description and imagery. I teach them to be clear and not just self-expressive. Other scientists must know what you mean, so having a strong command over language is pinnacle." Kamau took a big bite out of his burger. He was hungry … and pleased that the food was as good as the conversation.

"That's what's up." A light bulb went off for Shaka. "You know, when I hear them singing and rapping in the building, I often ask them what they think the songs mean to see if they really have a clue to what songs are talking about, and then I ask questions that will tell me if they believe the song to be a good example for them or a bad example. Most seem to get that most of the songs are not intended for them." Shaka laughs. "But I agree that using HipHop and other genres of music in the classroom is a good tool to use *IF you do it right*. Despite what most may think about it, sometimes kids today are learning more about life from HipHop than I can ever teach them because they listen to it a lot when they are away from school. HipHop is definitely a tool of self-expression, so I love how you use it. I mean, they will only listen to it any way; why not use it to help them?"

Kamau nodded in agreement, "Hmhmm!" His mouth was full with a mixture of onion rings and hamburger, but his ears were open, and his mind was enlivened. He swallowed his food and shared, "Here's an example: you got a young man, he cracks jokes, he talks throughout the whole day. Okay, great, guess what? He has a skill. That skill is verbal. It doesn't necessarily have to be cracking jokes, but he is verbally blessed. He could be the next great speaker in the world. We don't know because we haven't harnessed it. We don't take the time because it's disrupting our normal flow of things, but the last time I checked, school wasn't about creating a comfort for the teachers; it's about the teachers creating comfort for the student. So we gotta step out our comfort zone and comfort other people. HipHop is about evolution, transformation, and being able to survive. Many of the messages are about that—even today. I find popular HipHop tracks, that I know they love, take the instrumentals, and we create lyrics based upon the concept that was going on in the lesson. In Language Arts, I start off by creating the first lines of the lyrics that are based upon the lesson. Then, I give them an opportunity to write the bridge. We'll work collaboratively to take the content, write out a song, and then we perform it to some HipHop music. We sit there and make entire songs about global warming and stuff like that. That's another way I blend it, and what's remarkable is not only are they having fun with it, but they actually *understand* the science concept, and they start teaching the younger kids in the school! And so I use HipHop in all kinds of ways. It's remarkable the stuff that kids own and take away, and it's definitely had a great impact on the entire school community." Kamau popped an onion ring in his mouth as if he were rewarding himself.

Shaka nodded his head, dipped his last cheese stick in the small container of marinara sauce, and took a bite. He was deep in thought. He liked the idea of utilizing HipHop in the classroom, but he needed more than just engagement tips; he needed to connect with his students on a deeper level. Anybody can watch something, but you learn through the processing and the seeing and the pulling apart of words on a page. That was a big thing for him; he liked to see kids reading. When his students walk in the classroom, and they're like, "Can we get a little free time today?" after they've had an assembly or something that broke the day apart or they had a field trip where classes are kind of broken and staggered apart, he'd ask, "You got a book?" and they'd go, "Oh yes, yes. I've got it in my bag." He loved that feeling because he knew that much of what his kids see on TV, in the movies, in videos, and on social media is actually going on in their community. He wanted to equip his students back in North Carolina with critical thinking skills to help them navigate the harsh life that lay ahead of many of them; anything else would be a disservice.

Kamau chewed his food, swallowed, and continued, "When I'm administering the EOGs, the kids can't talk, but at the end—when everybody's sitting here I'm walking through the classroom, I'm rapping to a song in my head, and I'm bouncing to the beat, and the kids are just dying laughing without laughing out loud. Next thing you know, they're joining in. Everybody's bouncing to the same beat I'm bouncing to. They have no idea what song I'm singing in my head, but they're all bouncing to my beat."

Shaka turned and looked at Kamau. "Not *that's* a connection, Man!" Shaka exclaimed. He articulated, "That's really powerful. You've got me thinking about how I can more intentionally use HipHop as both a tool to engage students and as a tool to help students understand that we need to expand our minds. Everything that we put in our system is gonna come back to us in some way, shape, or form, so I want to help them understand positive HipHop and even talk more with them about the music that's not so positive—ya know, help them develop a critical lens. And I'm thinking this is a good way to expose them to different cultures of music because I just don't want my students to become single-minded in their music intellect. HipHop can be our connection to taking these youth much further, but we cannot fall victim to it either."

"Word," Kamau said. He checked his phone. The most recent alert indicated that his flight was scheduled to leave on time, which was in just under 45 minutes. He couldn't believe how fast the time had flown. He signaled Nia to bring their checks, looked at Shaka, and declared, "Bro, we all have stories. I share mine with my kids because they need to know that my struggle may be with a different generation, but not much has changed in the struggle. HipHop was wild back then, too. I saw the booty shaking, heard the cursing, saw the guns, saw the drugs, saw rappers slain, but I made it through the streets of NYC because I had help. I cannot say that I was unscathed because I definitely made some bad choices and got caught up in circumstances by being in the wrong areas at the wrong time. The greatest thing that I can do is to be honest with them. These kids love you when they know that you are real with them."

Kamau and Shaka stood up at the same time. Shaka read "7:32" on his watch and offered Kamau his hand to shake. He said, "Man, it's been a real honor meeting and kicking it with you today. We need to keep in touch." Shaka handed Kamau his business card. He nodded to Nia, "I got this." He gave her his credit card.

Kamau put Shaka's business card in his wallet, gave Shaka one of his business cards, and laughed, "I was going to get the bill, Man. Thanks though. You're a good brother. Your students are blessed to have you."

"Likewise, Man," Shaka shook his head, "You have no idea how you've impacted me today. You have a great flight, ahight."

"Say less. Enjoy your flight," Kamau smiled at Shaka as they walked in opposite directions toward their respective gates. What a moment! What an empowered experience to have as part of his conference travels. He couldn't wait to tell his students about it when he returned. He knew they would love to hear about it, and he wanted them to know that grown-ups make friends, too. As he approached his gate, he saw police with drug-sniffing dogs at the door to the jetway. They had pulled a twenty-something Black man with short locs aside and were going through his luggage. He laughed to himself and shook his head, not because anything was funny; he just wondered when they would ever have some relief from the surveillance of police.

CHAPTER 10
Inauguration Day

"It was all a dream!" The Notorious B.I.G. exclaimed as Kamau closed his laptop. He stood up. After the music stopped, he completed Biggie's thought in a quiet but clear voice, "I used to read *Word Up!* magazine"[75] as he stood in front of the full-length mirror on the back of his office door, adjusted his beige button up shirt and brown leather belt, then fixed his tie. He glanced at the digital calendar on his wall: Thursday, January 20, 2033—11:52 a.m. Mr. Miller had been preparing for his weekly after-school professional development session, but first, he needed to get through the day. He had a full house right now: everyone at Derrick Bell Elementary School (and the surrounding community) was just a few steps away watching the Presidential Inauguration. As he left his office and walked down the hallway to the auditorium, he was greeted by smiling children and parents, grandparents, aunts, and uncles—all there to be part of history. This inauguration was historic, not because it was a first but because it marked a serious shift in American politics. After President Joe Biden's unfortunate passing on January 15, 2027, Vice President Kamala Harris succeeded as President of the United States: the first woman president and the second self-identified person of color to sit in the Oval Office. After President Harris was reelected to serve an additional term, Hill Harper earned the seat. Kamau recalled the day the American people had elected their third person of color as President, and Black people all over the country were feeling the shift. The shift was so distinct, in fact, that it often felt like a dream to Kamau. Here he was watching the inauguration of President-Elect Hill Harper, the 48th President of the United States on a large screen in an auditorium filled with children, their families, their teachers, and school staff. Like President Obama back in 2009, President Harper appeared cool as a cucumber—like he was ready for the challenge. However, Kamau remembered how much grief White Americans gave President Obama during his two terms and how horribly sexist they were during President Harris' terms. He imagined how stressful the job of President could be. He hoped that *this* election was a sign that White Americans were *finally* coming around. He didn't imagine that they had arrived at a post-racial society because he knew there could never be such a thing, but he did hope to see continued progress across the racial divide.

President Harper's voice wavered as he repeated the Presidential oath, "I do solemnly swear …" he paused to clear his throat and continued, "that I will faithfully execute the Office of President of the United States, and will to the best of my ability, preserve, protect and defend the Constitution of the United States."[76] The new Black President now appeared a bit more nervous than he did a few minutes ago. Kamau was nervous for him. He was also nervous with him. Today was his first day hosting such a large crowd as the new principal of Derrick Bell Elementary School. He had been in this role since July, but since then, he's only held audience with the children who attend his school and his staff. So today was so big; in fact, it was huge. And the job of Principal felt huge, huge like President.

He had so many people looking to him—some were depending on him, and others were waiting to see if he would fail, and he felt the eyes … at all times. Finally peeling his eyes off the large screen at the back of the auditorium stage, he looked around the auditorium at his community. He loved that school, and he was sincerely honored to be leading it. As the new president completed his inaugural address, the entire auditorium roared with cheers and applause. Most in attendance were standing and high fiving one another, so he used that as his cue to walk to the front of the stage, stand behind the mic'd podium, and motion the crowd to quiet down. He cleared his throat and smiled at his community, "What an amazing day today is! And I am so glad you are here. Welcome! My name is Mr. Kamau Miller, and I am proud to be the Principal of Derrick Bell Elementary School here in *The* historic Hill District."

The crowd cheered, "Yay! Mr. Miller!" several community members, who were also his former students, shouted. The rest of the crowd laughed.

"Thank you so much. It is great to see so many of you here today to celebrate this momentous occasion in our country. President Hill Harper, like his predecessor President Harris, and her predecessor, President Obama, are shining, living examples of the magic that exists inside each of us. I started my career as a third-grade teacher in this very building." His former students applauded; the crowd laughed again. Mr. Miller chuckled briefly and continued, "I have been blessed to have a career in which I could bring together the entire community to be a force and a movement for young people. This room is full today, and not *just* because we were streaming the inauguration ..." A low giggle filled the auditorium. He continued, "But because you have demonstrated time and time again that Derrick Bell has a special magic. Thanks to you, we have a great mentoring program and a vibrant robotics program. Our young people are thriving because they enjoy being in the classroom and doing the things that the adults in this room and in this community have made possible for them to do." He stepped back from the podium and applauded his audience.

They joined him in filling the large room with applause.

Principal Miller stepped back up to the sleek, clear plastic podium, held onto the top with both hands, and asserted, "In all the years that I have been in education, I've learned a lot, and we have done really incredible work here. Since I have taken the reigns as principal, I am grateful to work with ... I mean, just an *amazing* staff, who are scholars, families and community members who I love, and I know love me back."

"We love you, Mr. Miller!" shouted a voice from the back of the auditorium. The crowd laughed at his supportive hecklers.

"And I love you back!" Mr. Miller responded. "Like President Obama—many of you might be too young to remember how smooth he was—President Harper is a cool dude. He has a swagger that cannot be denied.

And like that swagger, there is a rhythm to being part of a school community like ours. It has taken a few months, and it might take another year or two, but we are figuring out our rhythm together. I thank you for that." Kamau applauded his community members again, and they joined him.

He continued, "I loved teaching your children, and I love leading this school community. It has been a journey. The beautiful, talented, brilliant children at DBE deserve the very best, and that comes down to resources and everyone understanding that we are part of a *community*: one that is resource rich, one with folks who really care about this school's mission, are driven by our mission, and folks who decide to stand alongside the school while it matures into the school that we all know it can be! I am bent on ensuring that our young people, who have been historically marginalized in society, have the best opportunities and access to the best resources we can afford. Our children deserve the same if not more than their White counterparts."

"So what does that look like, Mr. Miller?" asked a voice from the left side of the room. Kamau looked in the direction of the voice, and the woman stood up. It was Ms. Clara, Mikhail's mother. Mr. Miller smiled. Mikhail had always been his favorite, most challenging student, and even though he was now a freshman in college, his mother remained active in the Derrick Bell Elementary School Parent Teacher Association.

"Thank you for that important question, Ms. Clara. It's good to see you here this morning. Give that young man a big hug for me, okay?" Mr. Miller started. Ms. Clara smiled, nodded, and sat down.

He continued, "What this looks like is having a very strong, full-service school that focuses on ensuring students have access to a full range of social and emotional resources in addition to a top-tier academic program. It means we now have a full-service infirmary, staffed by a full-time nurse. It means having formal relationships with strong community partners who provide mental health counseling and employment counseling. For students and families going through transitions or going through crisis, it means that we're not just helping the student, we're helping the family unit as a whole. It looks like the partner that I just confirmed yesterday who will fund our new global, social justice focused music program in which every student in this school, from PreK to 5th grade, will learn how to play a string instrument and become part of an orchestra."

"Wait a minute, Mr. Miller!" Niani interrupted. She was one of the former students who cheered for him earlier. She added, "That is all the way wild. We did not have anything like that when we were students here." She tapped Nasara, who was sitting next to her. They nodded at one another in agreement.

Mr. Miller nodded along with his two former students, "I know. I know. And it all comes down to the resources, the information, and having the access to people in this incredible community who have the means or are connected to people of means and have the ability to complement the state funding we receive. The additional dollars that come through philanthropy simply help us to do more. It's a real game changer."

The crowd applauded. As Kamau looked around the room, he saw smiling faces, and he was pleased. He had been anxious about this day, but so far—so good. Then, he noticed Ms. Dilsey, a third-grade teacher standing on the wall at the end of the front row. She quietly tapped her watch, alerting her principal that it was time to get the children back to their classrooms so that they could eat lunch. He nodded at her.

Kamau faced his community and shared, "Okay, everyone, I've been informed that it's time for me to be quiet and let you go on with your day, so let me say this last thing. This has been a faith walk. We have had some really incredible guardian angels who have made it possible for Derrick Bell Elementary School to do the things that we are currently doing." He paused and cleared his throat. "One of the things that I have learned in my time as a school leader is that each school community is different. There is always a group of people who care deeply about the mission and just want young people, their teachers, their families, and the community to thrive. Another thing I've learned is that people want to know, one …" he held up one finger, "Are you who you say you are? and two" he put up a second finger, "Are you walking the talk?" He put his hand down, looked around at the children sitting in the front half of the auditorium, and continued, "I know it takes time to get used to a new principal." He looked back at the community members gathered in the back half of the auditorium, "I know some people are expecting me to depart quickly because they think I am not going to stay long. I know that my predecessors have been much older than me and have brought a level of sage in the space, ... but I understand this community, I respect your needs, and I definitely understand that I am very unorthodox and incredibly different than what you've experienced in the past, so you may not understand how I move or *how* I show up for your children and this community. But I want everyone in this room today to know that my love for this community goes hard, and I understand that it will take some time to conquer some of your doubts. However, I am here to tell *them*" he stretched his arm straight to his right, pointing at the people outside of their community who do not believe in or support the families of color in the Hill, "a new story—that *we* are *the best* school in Pittsburgh, the best school in Pennsylvania, the best school in this country, and we are going to keep saying that until we get there!" The crowd burst into applause and stood on their feet. The children cheered and raised their fists in the air, a motion Mr. Miller had taught them the first week of school to show their Black pride. He walked around the front of the auditorium holding his fist high in the air and cheered with his students. The moment was magical!

"Whew!" he continued, "I am committed to Derrick Bell Elementary School. I believe in you, children; and I believe in this community. We are powerful, and we can accomplish any and everything we set our minds to."

He reached out toward the back of the auditorium with both arms, "Thank you for celebrating the inauguration of the *third* Black President of the United States with us today. I invite you into this building any time. The doors are always open to our community. Please join me in front of the stage, after we close, if you have any questions. And children, you keep up the amazing work. I am so, so, so proud of you. Let's have an unapologetically positive day! Please turn your attention to your teachers for your class's dismissal instructions."

Mr. Miller stepped away from the podium while smiling and applauding his children. He mentally prepared to field lots of individual questions and comments by the community members in attendance. As eager and inquisitive community members gathered around the new principal, the primary grade teachers moved closer to their respective classes and delivered instructions, and the upper grade teachers signaled for their students to be patient while the younger children exited the auditorium. Once the last primary class had left the room, the third- through fifth-grade teachers directed their classes to stand, and they filed out of the auditorium.

Principal Miller spent about 20 minutes answering questions and addressing the concerns shared with him that afternoon. The questions were many, but thankfully, the concerns were minor. As Mr. Miller stood in the middle of the small crowd, engaging the families of his children, Mr. Wilson, the third-grade all-boys' class teacher, caught his attention. He had returned to the auditorium after delivering his students to their Art teacher for Art class. He had scheduled time to meet with the new principal for a mid-year check-in during his prep period.

"Excuse me, everyone," Mr. Miller asserted, "I am sincerely grateful for your engagement and passion for our school. I hope I have answered all of your questions. If not, please contact Mrs. Frank in the front office to schedule an appointment so that I can give you the undivided attention your concern deserves. I do need to get back to my office now for a one o'clock meeting. While you are here, please feel free to visit classrooms and see what magical things your children are doing. Please get home safely." The community members obliged, thanked Mr. Miller again for the information he shared this morning, and left the auditorium.

Principal Miller looked at Mr. Wilson with raised eyebrows and took a deep breath.

Mr. Wilson handed his principal a bottle of water and asked, "You did well. You good?"

"Yeah" Mr. Miller sighed, "Thanks." He held up the water bottle before taking the cap off and drinking half the bottle. "Walk with me. How is your school year going? How is Derrick Bell treating you this year?" The two men walked side-by-side down the hall toward the Principal's Office.

"Mr. Miller," Mr. Wilson started, "Being the third-grade all-boys' teacher is one of the my favorite jobs ever. I mean, I really like being an all-boys' teacher."

Mr. Miller smiled as he swallowed another gulp of water, "That's wonderful news. I'm really glad to hear that you're feeling good in your position. I taught that class myself about 10 years ago." Mr. Miller held the door to his office open for Mr. Wilson to enter. The two men sat down at the round conference table in the right corner of the office. Mr. Miller grabbed his laptop off his desk, opened it, and sat it on the table in front of him. As he logged in and pulled up his Mid-Year Meeting (MYM) record so that he could take notes of the discussion, he said, "Tell me what you like most about teaching the all-boys class."

Mr. Wilson's face lit up. He replied, "It's having the opportunity to give back and to be a role model, a vehicle for our boys to explore what it means to be boy or male. I like being able to create an environment in which they know they are recognized as whole beings. I look at each boy in my class, and I recognize that I mean so much to each of them—all 29 of these boys, and that's a lot of testosterone," the two of them laughed, and Mr. Wilson shrugged, "which works for me."

Mr. Miller asserted, "Mr. Wilson, when I taught that class, part of the magic for me was being able to create the kind of environment that I needed when I was that age. I needed someone who cared about me and looked like me."

"Exactly!" Mr. Wilson concurred excitedly. He really enjoyed working with Mr. Miller, but this was their first time sitting down one-on-one, and he was glad that he was seen. "Mr. Miller, that's exactly it. At this age, they need rich, culturally relevant and sustaining curriculum experiences. They need to see themselves in the literature as protagonists as well as antagonists. They need to read stories that are driven by characters that look like them and act like them."

"I love the way your classroom sounds from the hall—so busy, so active," Mr. Miller stated.

"Thank you, Mr. Miller. I'm glad to hear that!" Mr. Wilson had been nervous about the levels of noise that often come from his room. "It's an organized chaos." He shared proudly. "How I set-up my classroom may have bothered other teachers because it could look like they're all over place, they're just doing a whole bunch of random stuff, and they're making all this noise. But I encourage you or anyone to come in and ask any of my students what they're doing. They can tell you the purpose, why they're doing what they're doing, what they're talking about. They know how long they have in regard to getting things accomplished. They know what they're working towards because it's not just about the individual reward in my class; it is also a collective journey. I design the environment to say, *This is us—our classroom family. This is what we do.* And I think that it is important for them to have these kinds of structures in place as well as lots of creative lesson planning."

Mr. Miller nodded his head as he jotted some notes on his virtual form. "Indeed, indeed, Mr. Wilson. I love how you have designed your classroom environment. You are happy. Your boys appear happy. They're doing well academically and socially. I know you've taught co-ed classes before though. Talk to me about the difference. Is the biggest difference for you the creative lesson planning you mentioned, classroom set-up, engagement, or something else?"

Mr. Wilson sat forward in his chair and responded, "Well, I can modify any of my lesson plans to meet the needs of a single-gender or co-ed space. I think it's just the strategies I use. It's the engagement tools. It is how I galvanize their attention in regard to how they are showing up. The tools are fairly transferable, but what I've learned was when I see a young man who is displaying particular energies—he may be angry, he might be anxious, maybe have a particular feeling—I know how to engage that energy, and I also know how to give him space. I think that's the biggest difference."

"Nice, Nice. That makes sense, Mr. Wilson. Have you had any experiences with students who you feel particularly benefitted from being in the all-boys' class?" Mr. Miller asked.

Mr. Wilson shook his head, "Oh absolutely. I have one boy who, at the beginning of the year, everyone had a negative story about him, including the AP. And I'm like, so here's a young man who is a third grader who's reading on a kindergarten level, and you all are making fun of him. He had actually repeated twice, which means that we have failed him collectively. But I was failing him as well, until I found creative ways to reach him by actually showing him that I care, by being patient with him, by demonstrating resilience, and by really strategic teaching. I helped him find the confidence to be able to read and thrive in school. And I think that I did okay with helping him to co-create a new narrative of himself because by December, he was showing signs of being an incredible mathematician. That was the thing that he was absolutely solid at, and once he started to experience success in a supportive environment, he discovered that he could actually read too!"

"Well, look at that! We're talking about George, right? You've done a really incredible job with him. He's come such a long way." Mr. Miller asked.

Mr. Wilson nodded affirmatively, "Thank you, Mr. Miller, but it wasn't just me. He had to participate and make the tough decision that he was going to engage in this different way of being, and once we were all on the same page, it was phenomenal. I mean, all 29 boys pulled together to build that environment. They just support one another, with friendly competition."

Mr. Miller was really enjoying this MYM. He had MYMs scheduled with each of his teachers, and he looked forward to the opportunity to check in with each of them individually to learn more about them and their teaching styles. He asked, "Mr. Wilson, I know you do a lot of project-based learning with your students. What is one of the most formidable projects that you all have completed so far this school year?"

Mr. Wilson smiled, "Definitely our DBE Presidential Election! This being the *first* year President Harper was up for a presidency, we held a school-wide election. The boys had to man the polls, they had to create the election ballots. They were the ones who counted the ballots. They were the ones who ran the campaigns. They did all of it to coordinate and get their fellow students and staff in and out of space to vote and tally, and then present the results to the school community. The reason why it was formidable for them is because these boys have already been counted out in the community, and they have been counted out many times over. So … when they were able to execute this, they were so proud of themselves, and they were able to take on other projects that involved community service: you know they actually ran the food pantry. I have plans to continue taking them on field trips all year because I don't think any teacher has taken them anywhere. My goal is to take them on 9 field trips this year—one each month to places and for experiences that integrate everything that we're learning in class. I want them to go see their curriculum in action. I need to make sure they know it's real, and they're living history."

Mr. Miller responded, "I love that. You guys really did a great job with that election project. You impacted not just your children, but the entire school. All of the children got involved and learned a lot. Thank you for doing that work so creatively and hands-on. Also, I do love your field trip idea, and I fully support it as long as each excursion is directly connected to your curriculum." Kamau looked up from the keyboard at his colleague, "What are your long-term professional goals, Mr. Wilson? Where do you see yourself in 5 years? 10 years?"

Mr. Wilson sat back in the chair and looked Mr. Miller in the eyes, "I see you. I see how you move and interact with the children, the staff, and the community. You haven't even been here a full school year, and you've already made so much happen for us. Watching you, and how you've changed this school for the better, has really got me thinking about administration. What inspired *you* to move from the classroom to the front office?"

Mr. Miller was pleased that Mr. Wilson had noticed such positive attributes in his behavior. He was passionate about inspiring and working with other Black men in education, so Mr. Wilson's question was music to his ears. He sat back away from his laptop and shared, "Okay, so first, I never could have done any of what I've done alone. I love working with others—other teachers, community folk. Children are amazing, and I've been blessed to work with people who are committed to serving children. When I think about why I moved from the classroom to the front office …, I just knew that it had to be done differently. I had faced and experienced some models of principalship and leading that weren't … they weren't nurturing to me, and I was like, well, what if I have the ability to actually take what I've been able to do in my classroom and do it on a broader scale?"

"I can believe that," Mr. Wilson responded. "What steps did you take once you decided you wanted to be an administrator? What was it like?"

Kamau looked at Mr. Wilson, "I'll keep it all the way real with you. I decided, all right, let me see if I have what it takes to do this thing, so I took some gambles. No one teaches you this—like I got my master's degree in school administration—but no one tells you that it's different when you're in it. People can tell you how it is for them all day, you can take all the classes you want, but when you're in it, it's a different feel. I took some leadership courses. I completed 2 years as a principal intern in 2 different school communities. I also took part in 2 different district-sponsored school leadership programs: they're for anyone who's aspiring to be a principal or AP. I would definitely recommend that for you. And in my second year as a principal intern, I got an email from the superintendent's office. It bugged me out. I thought I was in trouble!" They laughed then Kamau continued, "She said that she'd been watching me for a while. She'd been watching how I was moving across the city because I wasn't just teaching in the classroom. She saw that I was in the community doing work, and that my students were thriving as well: academically, socially and emotionally. She had heard from district-level people who had come to my classroom to see me work my magic. She told me she felt that I had strengths in relationship building, that people trusted me because I knew how to say the things that needed to be said. Then, she asked me if I believed that I could transfer that spirit and energy into running a school. It took a second for me to get really comfortable with it all, but here I am." He threw his hands up and looked around his office, slapped his hands down on his thighs, and looked at Mr. Wilson.

"That's a powerful story, Mr. Miller. You straight up walked the talk and manifested this position for yourself. I like that. Do you think you can mentor me as I figure out my next steps?" Mr. Wilson asked his principal.

Mr. Miller smiled, "Most certainly, Mr. Wilson. I'll be honored to support your journey into administration. I've had a number of guardian angels, and if I can come anywhere close to that for you, it would be a true honor." Kamau placed both his hands on the table as if he were about to stand up. Then, he relaxed back into his seat and turned to Mr. Wilson, "When I was named Principal, I got a phone call from this gentleman named Dr. Charles Anderson. He is an upper-level administrator in the district. We would have weekly calls: he would talk to me about what it meant to be a Black male leader. I learned so much from him in 6 months, and I'm still learning a lot from him. It is how he shows up, how he demonstrates a sense of *Here's the vision, here's what we need to do in order to execute the vision*, and he's taught me how to allow myself to be vulnerable and how to create safe spaces for my staff and students. I've shadowed him having tough conversations with his staff. He'll be like, *I gotta close this door, we're gonna talk. It's gonna be hard. I'm letting you know the conversation is gonna be tough, but when we come out of it, I still got your back, still believe in you, but we gotta do some things differently.* It is one of the most impactful relationships I've ever had, so I know the power of mentoring, and I am looking forward to walking this walk with you, Mr. Wilson."

Mr. Wilson smiled. He felt seen and heard. Even better, he felt supported. He responded, "I was a bit nervous walking in here today, but now, knowing that I have a Black male leader who is with me on this journey, makes me feel much better. Thank you for your support, Mr. Miller."

"You're very welcome, Mr. Wilson. This has been a great Mid-Year Check-in. Thank you for your time and all of the great work you are doing with the children. I'll see you in the Technology Center for PD afterschool." Mr. Miller was so full from his meeting with Mr. Wilson that he almost didn't notice his phone vibrating on his desk.

As Mr. Wilson left the office, Kamau sat at his desk and reached for his new AfroBeats 7000 smartphone. His Beloved had just bought them both new matching phones, and Kamau was still getting used to the settings. He remembered her being so excited to support 50 Cent's newest enterprise: the first Black-owned smartphone company. She was such the 50 aficionado, that she had enthusiastically preordered the first model, the AfroBeats 5000, before they even hit the streets in July of 2030. As he tapped the icon to take the call, he admired his beautiful family on the home screen: his incredible wife of 8 years, Diane, and their delightful twin daughters, Gazi and Elon.

"Hey there, Beloved," Kamau said as he answered the phone. He had been calling Diane *Beloved* since the day she moved back to Pittsburgh after graduating from her master's program. That was also the day he proposed. They got married on August 5, 2025, and he was grateful to have found his person.

"My Sweet," Diane responded, "How's your day been?" She didn't always call her husband during the day, but she had a break in between clients and wanted to share something with him.

"I'm good, Baby." Kamau answered, taking a deep breath. "It's been an amazing day—incredible and empowering. What did you think of the Inauguration?"

"Oh, it was beautiful. I love that we can look forward to that day now. I am still in shock that Black bodies have occupied the White House now on *three* separate occasions! Harper was smooth, and First Lady Mrs. Regina King Harper was absolutely flawless and stunning! But that's not why I called you." She interrupted herself, "Listen, we just listened to a wonderful episode of this podcast by Nas with Mary J. Blige. One of the other Advocates here put it on. Their conversation *was so amazing*. The name of the podcast is *The Bridge*: *50 Years of HipHop,* and he had a really great conversation with Mary J. about what the early days were like. It was very similar to what Jemele Hill does on her podcast, and the question was *when did you become unbothered? And how did you feel that you could be authentic and just risk and do your thing*? Nas talked about how being on the street required him to have a level of overconfidence that was necessary in order to get the job done, especially in the environment that he was in. He felt that was something he owed to himself as well as his audience. I'm saying, Babe, that's what I love about HipHop: just being unapologetic about owning your walk for the world. So I thought of you while you're at school today because I feel like that's incredibly important to pour into our youth. It's hard for them to realize that you can be unapologetic and be yourself. I see it all the time in this environment we're in, especially with social media, how it drives things. You might carry that confidence for about 15 minutes but not necessarily for the actual duration of your walk and journey." Diane shook her head on the end of her AfroBeats 7000.

Kamau agreed, "Yeah, I feel for these children because social media shapes so much of their experience, and it takes so long for that message to sink in to the point where it really resides within them, you know?"

"I do … unfortunately, I do." Diane concurred, "Wait, hold on, Babe. Excuse me?" Someone in Diane's office started talking to her. She listened for a few seconds, then came back to the phone, "Okay, Babe, I gotta tend to something. I love you. Have a great PD this afternoon."

"Thanks for the call, Beloved. You take it easy over there," Kamau responded.

Kamau hung up his phone and placed it in the wooden upright smartphone holder that one of his students made for him so that he could see the photo of his family. He loved the connection he had with Diane—their beautiful Black family, their mutual love for HipHop, and their passion for serving others. It was everything he ever desired in a family. The time on his screen read 2:27 p.m. "Wow. This day has flown by," he thought, "to the Tech Center I go to mold adult minds." He picked up his phone, laptop, and water bottle, then headed out of his office to set up for the after-school session with his teachers.

By the time Kamau reached the school's Tech Center, his staff was already gathered. It was 2:45 p.m. The children had been dismissed for the day, and several family members had stopped him in the hall to share how happy they were to have him at the school and how grateful they were that he hosted an Inauguration Party that morning. He loved engaging with his students' families, and he was excited about this afternoon's PD. Mrs. Frank was there arranging the room and setting up the technology. She smiled and gently took the laptop from him and synced it to the projector as Mr. Miller took a few minutes to greet and talk with a few of the teachers gathered in the front of the room.

"Thank you, everyone, for a truly wonderful day!" He began. "I know that our school was really busy today, so thank you for being so present and attentive to the community members who were in the building today and for so actively engaging our children in today's inauguration. After our fall election," Mr. Miller looked at Mr. Wilson sitting in the back of the room, "led by the third grade all-boys class, our children had a vested interest in this historic moment, so I believe today was a powerful culmination of all that they have been learning and doing. Thank you for that. Now, this afternoon, we're going to do a few things," He pointed to the agenda on the screen. "First, we'll talk about you. I want to be clear about what your needs are from me. Next, we'll talk about how we can better leverage music and social media in the classroom. And for the last activity, I've been asked by the superintendent to tell her what your overarching needs are, so … we'll close with a discussion on that. Okay?"

The teachers nodded their heads.

"First," Mr. Miller began, "I want you to know that I understand the story that's visible in the classroom; I also understand the story that's *not* being visible. I understand your journey. When I walk into your classrooms, I want you to trust that my lens is broad and comprehensive. I am *not* here for *The Gotcha*. I am invested in your well-being, in the building and strengthening of your craft, and I am willing to work with you through the tough stuff—stuff that is sometimes beyond the scope of your role. So please communicate your needs and concerns with me so that we may be in partnership and collaboration with one another." He paused and looked around the room to see if there were any questions or comments. The teachers looked pleased, seemed engaged, and interested in what he might say next, so he continued, "Next, it is clear that there are a lot of things that are really working well here that we can build on. Let's talk for a few moments about how we can build momentum on the awesome learning that is happening at DBE. Ms. Penolia?"

Ms. Penolia and the other teachers started to share the different learning activities they were doing in their respective classrooms, and the room was abuzz as the teachers worked collaboratively to identify ways to take the good things they were already doing and make them even better.

Kamau walked around the room and engaged teachers as they talked in grade-level groups about new ideas for experiential learning activities in the spring. Since before the winter break, he had noticed an increased need for validation among his teachers. Some of them were already feeling burned out, so he wanted to find ways to reinvigorate them. He believed that started with validating who they were as human beings as well as who they wanted to see themselves being as teachers. When they returned from the winter break, he had started randomly leaving personal notes for teachers on their desks or sending quick emails that said things like, "Thank you for being present today. I know it's not always easy. Please come to my office and pick up some *Just Because I Appreciate You* snacks." On about four different occasions this month, he had stepped into classrooms and said to the teacher, "Listen, why don't you take a break? I got it. I'd like to do an activity with your children" or "I'll take them to recess," or wherever else they needed to go. He found that kind of hands-on compassionate approach to supporting his teachers was important. It helped them to feel seen. He found that leading a school required a lot of magic, but he was here for it. His days were full and sometimes hectic, but he was committed to going above and beyond to help his children and staff be the best humans they could be.

After the teachers had wrapped up their initial discussion and entered their discussion notes in the shared digital spreadsheets, Mr. Miller said, "Thank you for a great discussion. I'm excited about what the last half of this school year will look like. Now, social media and music. This is an on-going conversation in the district and in our community. I am committed to continuing the work that we are doing here, but I want us to have some conversation about *how* we are thinking about these things and how we are using them in the class. Since I want everyone to be actively involved in this conversation, I'll set the laptop to transcribe your sharings." Kamau activated the "Transcribe" option on his laptop.

The third-grade all-girls' teacher, Ms. Dilsey, jump-started the conversation, "My girls and I were just creating vision boards, and one of the girls added a picture of Lizzo's *Special*[77] album cover. During her presentation, the girls had a great discussion about some of Lizzo's history as an artist. That album came out 11 years ago, and my students discussed a timeline of her social media posts about all of the negative body-shaming and hatred that she had experienced over the years from folks on social media. Here's a grown woman who created a song that is an anthem designed to speak against all of what she had experienced on social media that has had such traction. It just shows how powerful social media was and still is. She's an incredible role model, an incredible performer, a true artist. She's a Black woman, a woman of size, who was inspired and created opportunities for so many other folks. She's a powerful advocate, and I'm like, if *she* is someone who has done all of this and is deeply impacted by all of the negative stuff that shows up on social media, how are our kids going to navigate this?"

Mr. Thompson, a second-grade mixed-gender class teacher added, "It's really hard, Ms. Dilsey. I'm trying to think like, *Okay, what is it that they can rely on? Is it something from Glorilla? is it Lady Leshurr? is it Toosii?* I'm wondering who is providing something that is going to reside within the spirit of our kids so that they don't give into social media and what social media is telling them. I feel like we've been fighting against media that drives children to places of darkness since the 2020 Shut Down. Art is hard."

The teachers nodded and shook their heads in a staggered unison, uttering words of agreement and concern.

Fifth-grade mixed-gender class teacher, Mrs. Frances, cleared her throat and sat up tall in her chair. The most senior teacher on the staff, Mrs. Frances had been at DBE since before Mr. Miller was first hired there as a third-grade teacher. She was preparing to retire when she received word that Mr. Miller had been hired as the new principal, so she deferred her retirement for another few years just to support and mentor him. She added, "Here's what the fifth grade teachers have been doing. We bring in the HipHop lyrics that drive our students: the clean lyrics, of course. Then, we talk about them. We talk about the poetics. We talk about the imagery. We talk about what people are using as tropes in order to grab their attention. We talk about the beef in HipHop—how you deal with someone putting you on Front Street, disrespecting you, and still save face. We have really rich and empowering discussions about how we leverage music and social media as we create a sense of self, while not allowing those things to drive us to make poor choices."

"Thank you for sharing the amazing work happening in the fifth grade, Mrs. Frances," Mr. Miller smiled at his mentor. "Thank you, Ms. Dilsey. I love that vision board activity and the ensuing discussion. Thank you, Mr. Anderson, for your thoughts as well. It is clear that we are actively helping our kids to think about what they're consuming, what they're digesting, how they are showing up in the world, and talking about why music makes them feel the ways it makes them feel. I encourage us to also include conversations about the objectification of gendered bodies, misogyny,[78] misogynoir,[79] and things like that because our children are hearing these terms all the time, and we want to make sure that we are keeping our minds open for safe and accurate exploration and understanding of these topics."

"Now, for our final task for this afternoon," Mr. Miller asserted, "I have been asked what your overarching needs are. There are 18 of you here, so I'd like us to work in 3 groups of 6. Please gather how you wish. In your groups," Mr. Miller points to the slide on the screen, "create a list of the things you need to help you better serve our children and the things you need to keep you in place at DBE. In other words, what can the district do to eliminate high turnover rates among teachers? and to attract more teachers of color, particularly Black men teachers? Then, I'd like for you to select a theme song that best conveys the overarching concept behind your list and share why you chose that song. Okay? Thoughts? Questions?" He paused for a few seconds and looked around at the smiling, but deep-in-thought teachers scattered around the Tech Center. "If not, please get to work in your groups, and let's take about 20 minutes for discussion." He set the digital timer on the screen.

The large room was alive with conversation and softly playing lo-fi music as the teachers worked in their three groups for the allotted time. Mr. Miller walked around the room engaging one group at a time for a few minutes, listening to their ideas, and answering their questions about the activity. As the timer ticked down, the teachers settled back into their seats. When the timer rang "0:00," Mr. Miller asked the teachers who would like to go first. Mrs. Frances, the selected leader of her group said, "We'd like to go first. Mr. Wilson is our Reporter." She looked at Mr. Wilson smiling proudly.

Surprised but clear not to question Mrs. Frances, Mr. Miller raised his eyebrows and looked toward the group's reporter. "Mr. Wilson?" Mr. Miller stepped toward the side of the room and motioned for Mr. Wilson to come to the front to share his list with the whole group.

Mr. Wilson started, "Okay. My group was made up of me, Mr. Thompson, Mr. London, Mrs. Frances, Ms. Henry, and Mr. John. Our theme song is *The Message* by Grandmaster Flash and the Furious Five. We feel that the lines *Don't push me 'cause I'm close to the edge. I'm trying not to lose my head*[80] really help convey the feeling behind our overall list. Why did we choose that song? Because we feel like they know exactly what to do to make us happy, to make us feel better about our jobs, but still they ask us this question. It's frustrating."

Mrs. Frances interrupted, "But we are obedient, so we did create a list." The group of teachers laughed.

Mr. Wilson laughed at his colleague, "I got you, Mrs. Frances." He pointed to their list on the screen, "Just so y'all know, we decided to focus on

Black men teachers, okay? Okay. Number one: *Recognize the Diamond you have in Black and Brown Men* who have made the conscious choice to educate young people."

A collective "Ooooohhh" rose from the room full of teachers.

Mr. Wilson continued, "Number two: *Nurture Male Teachers*. You also have to make sure that you are supporting male teachers by pairing them with mentors and people who can help them create community because it can feel—when you are a man of color in education, especially in elementary education—like you're out here by yourself." His colleagues nodded their heads in agreement.

He moved on to the next item on their list, "Number three: *Let Us Teach*. We feel that if a Black man does make a good teacher, then they're trying to pull you out of your class to be a dean or to become a principal, and you lose some of that *magic*—like Mr. Miller says—that you have when they are actually hands-on with young people. We're not saying don't support brothers who want to move out of the classroom. We're just saying don't push us out of the classroom." The teachers clapped quietly for number 3.

"You're doing an excellent job, Mr. Wilson," Mrs. Frances whispered to her colleague. He winked at her in appreciation of her encouragement.

"Number four," he continued, "*Connect Male Teachers to One Another*. We think that making sure male teachers, and Black male teachers especially, are connected to some entity like, Call Me Mr. MISTER or The Teachers' Lounge or He Is Me Institute,[81] is another way to drive Black male engagement, empowerment, and keep men in education. Number five: this one definitely benefits everyone, *Professional Development*. They should be making sure that we have continuous opportunities to grow our craft." His colleagues clapped again. The other teachers were loving Group One's list, and they loved that the list focused on Black men.

Mr. Wilson took a deep breath and stated, "Number six: *Financial Incentives*. Teaching is hard, and becoming a teacher can be expensive, so we should have access to tuition reimbursement programs and resources related to financial literacy because we have personal lives, and *that* can be expensive."

Ms. Dilsey added, "I know that's right!" The room filled with laughter.

Mr. Wilson smiled at his colleagues, looked at the screen, and continued, "Okay everyone, this is our last one. Lucky number seven: *Check and Manage the Racists*."

Another low "oooohhh" came over the room. Someone whispered, "Nice. They're not holding back at all."

Mr. Wilson looked at Mr. Miller, who was smiling, and finished sharing his group's list, "It's 2033, and there are *still* structures in place that perpetuate racist behavior. So … we were saying that we need them to create an environment in which there are very clear guidelines, restrictions, and repercussions on discrimination and aggressions—and we called them aggressions because there's nothing *micro* about the way they act and the things they say. Racism is painful, it digs deep and takes up residence in Black folk's spirits, and we've just had enough."

Mr. Miller initiated the applause for Group One. Their list was comprehensive and honest. He appreciated that. He was truly proud of his teachers for being so upfront with their needs, and he would be sure to compile their *complete* lists into one and share their thoughts with the superintendent. He felt good about having created a space in which teachers could openly share their concerns without any backlash. Inauguration Day was rounding out nicely, and he couldn't wait to hear the next two groups' presentations. Just then, Mrs. Frank, the Front Office Manager, stepped back into the Tech Center and called his name loudly and repeatedly, "Mr. Miller! Mr. Miller! Mr. Miller!"

Kamau looked up confused. He blinked. Through blurred eyes, he saw that he was not in the Derrick Bell Elementary School Technology Center standing in front of a room full of teachers. He was not a principal. He was seated in an aisle seat on an airplane about to land in Chicago, where he would be attending the Critical Race Studies conference. The flight attendant was attempting to awaken him so that he could adjust his back rest before landing. She called him again, "Sir, are you okay?"

He looked to his left at the two White women sitting next to him and to his right: three more White folks. "Damn," he said to himself, "It *was* all a dream."

Epilogue
A Love Letter to Black Men Teachers

Whether in an actual prison or not, practically every Black male in the United States has been forced at some point in his life to hold back the self he wants to express, to repress and contain for fear of being attacked, slaughter, destroyed.[82]

My Brothers,

The first time I read bell hooks' words, my heart sank. She had been a cerebral[83] othermother to me, guiding me on my transition to womanhood, facilitating my understanding of what it means to be Black, woman, and empowered. Moreover, she taught me that Black Feminism is a humanist project focused on resisting oppression and building, cultivating, and empowering the entire Black family, not man-hating. Her words assured me that there was nothing wrong with me loving Black men and that Black men deserved to be able to love, show love, and be loved. Therefore, the stories in this book are about love. They're also about HipHop, education, self-expression, passion, and empowerment because, to me, those things are forms of love. These stories come from you: Black men educators who dared to tell their truth to an individual Black woman looking to amplify their voices. I hope I have given your words justice.

Kamau Miller is the embodiment of you all. His journey throughout these pages spanned a full academic year. We cheered him on as he found love with a romantic partner and experienced BlackBoyJoy at the Rucker, baring his soul as he displayed his sincerely vulnerable heart. We sat with him as he prepared for a night out with his home boys, engaging in rich conversation about otherfathering in one of the safest spaces known to

Black men—the barbershop. We partied with Kamau as he discussed his reasons for teaching young children, inspiring another Black man to answer the call and follow his heart to the classroom. We cleaned up with Kamau as he discussed the upward battle that many Black male teachers face and some of the tangible ways they work to affect real change in today's schools. We traveled with Kamau as he rounded out his school year with a robust conversation on HipHop's place in the classroom and its role in encouraging students' creativity. Finally, we dreamed with Kamau. Regardless of the space he occupied or the people he met along the way, Kamau honored his passion for working with children. But not only did he consistently honor his passion, he also inspired others. That is what great teachers do: they ignite the spark in others to be more amazing than they ever believed they could be. Though Kamau is a composite character, he is very much real. He is very much who we desire to be. He is very much who we hope and pray will stand in front of our own children one day. Kamau is who we all strive to be. Kamau is you.

The last words spoken to me by the very first gentleman I interviewed follow:

> I'm glad this research is happening. It's integral to our community. It's integral to the education profession. Not enough people are doing it, so I'm glad that you're taking this on. And I look forward to seeing what's going to come about it because I've seen few books really focus in on male teachers of color who are in this, especially elementary teachers. We have secondary ed, but not too many people are interested in investing time and effort into this. And I think that it's time. It's time.—Mr. Caleb Mitchell[84]

Black men, you are worthy—worthy of our time, worthy of love, worthy of being your full selves, worthy of freedom. And to those of you brave enough to teach despite the stigma and the low pay, I salute you, I thank you, I love you.

Peace & Blessings,

Dawn

Afterword: Every [Black] Boy Needs a Little Love

Kamau and the Many Black Men Teachers

Cheryl E. Matias, PhD

Professor, University of San Diego

When Doechii sang "What It Is"[85] she calls us out on how Black folks are treated in America, particularly the Black men. As if Black men are nothing but thugs, criminals, or pariahs of the earth or, as Black psychologist. As Frantz Fanon once wrote, "nothing but dung heap."[86] In my lectures around the nation, I often cite Fanon's quotation at length because from it we, as a society, can hear how rooted anti-Blackness is in the racial fabric of the world. He uses the word "disgusting" to showcase how White supremacy has fostered a false love of Black men, simply because they are expected to bear the burden of work, discrimination, and generations of chattel slavery while being blamed for it all. So, when Doechii repeats "every block boy needs a little love,"[87] it becomes a sad prophetic tale of how Black men are treated in US society and never given the love they so deserve.

I, for one, am sick and tired of hearing news, media, and people quickly react to the beatings of Black men via the hundreds of viral videos capturing police brutality by saying nonsense like, "Well, he's a thug anyway." This dismissive tactic is just another maneuver of White supremacy because in their knee-jerk reaction to label all Black men a thug and thus worthy of a beating, even institutionalized murder. He avoids looking at their own inner racist: literally his own inner hate. Therefore, one can understand how refreshing it was to see a book about love: Black love. Not frilly romantic love nor a love that simply masks lust, but a humanly love that pushes back on the hateration of *what it is*.

Yet, what it is, is not always about hate because artifacts like this book, *The Journey of Kamau Miller: HipHop Composite Counterstories for Black Men Teachers*, is a testament of the love that Black men hold and how, in this case, Mr. Kamau Miller, a Black man teacher, shows love every day to his students. Dr. Hicks Tafari refreshingly uses her love for HipHop to translate boring, and oftentimes lifeless, White educational research into a colorful story of how one Black man refused to give up on Black students, claiming, "as long as I have breathe in my body … I'm gonna try to make sure that these young Black boys don't become a statistic." From stories of Kamau's upbringing with the love of his uncle Dez, to his interaction with students, Hicks Tafari gives to us what it is to love. She refuses to settle with the ethos of "it is what it is" and instead uses her research training to provide us with a *counterstory*[88] that simply counters the *mierda*[89] out there about Black men.

Drawing from generations of storytelling to highlight the morals, actions, and intentions of love, this book follows suit and is written entirely in conversational style. In doing so, it highlights Black customs and culture of storytelling, passing down the conversation of loving one another amidst unlovingness. A pattern so often reflected in the work of critical race theorist, Derrick Bell.[90] His work, alongside Dr. Hicks Tafari's, reminds us that words—Black words matter. That Black stories count. That Black love exists. And knowing that every Black boy needs a little love, I end with Mr. Miller's own words:

> part of my role is to show … my colleagues that an African American male teacher does have a right and can educate students … my role is to help other African American boys and men see that there's a future in education … to show that we belong here.

Yes, you do belong Mr. Miller. You and the many Black men and boys out there.

Pulling Back the Curtain

Much of the data utilized to birth Kamau Miller and craft the composite counterstories were gathered during a year-long study. My exploration into the lived experiences of Black men teachers served as an opportunity for me and my participants to unapologetically and rigorously make meaning together. As I set out on this exploratory journey, the following three overarching questions guided my inquisition:

1. What are the types of life experiences that shape Black men from the HipHop generation into elementary school teachers?
2. What inspires Black men to teach elementary school children despite the societal stigmas?
3. How does HipHop culture impact the identity development and pedagogy of Black men who become elementary school teachers?

I utilized a critical race methodology[91] to share these men's lives in a storied, culturally subjective manner. This method of research allowed me to garner a fuller understanding of the gentlemen's experiences. I encouraged my storytellers to use language to make sense of their lives, constructing stories as a way of sharing their personal experiences with me. As the narrator of this research, I did not assume any power. I did not strive to *give voice* to Black male teachers; they already have voices. What I did hope to do, however, was to hear their voices with my head and my heart and then offer critical interpretations of the stories they shared with me. I sought to broadcast their voices loudly and clearly, and hopefully, shed some light on the lives of these extraordinary men. My process was layered and multidimensional. I presented my research data in this text in the form of composite counterstories to make the work more accessible to people who do not have PhDs and may not understand all the fancy multisyllabic jargon that academicians like to throw around. However, I thought it might be helpful to my diverse readership if I shared what is behind the curtain for this work. The interview questions I created to guide my one-on-one interviews are included in Appendix A. Appendix B contains the Participants' Profile Chart for this study. This chart paints a picture of each of the men who contributed to this work. Of course, pseudonyms have been assigned to respect their anonymity. In Appendix C, I offer a more direct interpretation of my research—answers to my research questions because how fair would that be to tell you what my research questions are and then not answer them for you? The names that you will see in parentheses correlate with the names in the Participants' Profile Chart and are included to help you draw direct connections between the experiences and the gentlemen. I also referenced the specific gentlemen to help you further see how integrated the data are throughout *The Journey of Kamau Miller*. Next, in Appendix D, I offer what I believe to be a few possible implications for future research for those interested in extending and expanding this work. These implications are not all-inclusive and all-encompassing of every implication possible—just my thoughts about some possible jump-off points. Finally, in Appendix E, I share a list of resources for Black men teachers that I have gathered over the years. This is not an exhaustive list; this list can be used as a resource for Black men teachers to connect with other Black men in education, engage in professional development, and cultivate their overall amazingness.

Appendix A
Interview Questions

INITIAL INTERVIEW

1. Tell me about yourself.
2. In what ways did your experiences growing up as a student influence your desire to become a public school teacher?
3. What inspired you to become an elementary school teacher?
4. Tell me about the teachers who have had the most impact on your life.
5. What expectations did you have coming into the elementary school classroom?
6. What life experiences—prior to becoming a teacher—helped to shape these expectations?
7. What do you believe to be your role as an elementary school teacher?
8. Were your educational experiences different for you as a Black boy than they were for the Black girls?
9. Do you believe that the presence of Black male teachers in the elementary school classroom has an impact on boys? Please explain your response.
10. What are your favorite HipHop songs? Why?
11. Who are your favorite HipHop artists? Why?
12. Do you use HipHop in the classroom? Why or why not? If so, how?
13. Given that I am interested in Black men elementary school teachers, is there anything else that I might not have thought to ask you that you want to share?

FOLLOW-UP INTERVIEW

1. Tell me about what you are doing now.
2. How do you feel you have gotten to this point in your career?
3. What would you say is the biggest difference between public and charter schools?
4. What is it about teaching a single-gender classroom that really stands out to you?
5. What inspired you to go into administration?
6. What would you say to someone who is a teacher and wants to be an administrator that you feel would have made it for you to transition into that role?
7. Tell me about those people who inspired you or who mentored and supported you along the way.
8. What HipHop artists are you listening to right now?
9. Who are your favorite artists?
10. How can educators leverage social media to change the world?
11. Are you in touch with any of your former students?
12. What would you say to school districts and teacher education programs interested in increasing the number of Black male teachers?

Appendix B
Participants' Profile Chart

Name	Birth Year	Years of Experience in 2012	School Location (US)	School Type	Current Grade and Subject	Favorite HipHop Songs
Caleb Mitchell	1979	11 years	North East—large urban city	Public elementary	Fifth—all subjects	"If I Ruled the World"—Nas "Dear Mama"—Tupac "Jesus Walks"—Kanye West "It's a Good Life"—Kanye West
Shawn Wise	1976	12 years	Mid-Atlantic—large urban city	Public K–8	Fifth and sixth—math	"Anything"—OutKast "1986"—Big K.R.I.T. "High Definition"—Rick Ross "Ambition"—Wale
Victor Lucas	1984	1 month	South East—small rural town	Public elementary	Fifth math	"Juicy"—B.I.G. "Superfreak"—Jeezy "Spend It"—2 Chainz
Rob Porter	1987	1 year	South East—small rural town	Public elementary	Fourth—math	"Satisfy You"—Diddy "Don't Want to Waste Your Life"—Lecrae "Everything"—Canton Jones
Benjamin Robinson	1984	4 years	South East—large urban city	Public elementary	Pre-K—all subjects	"Motivation"—T.I. "Big Pimpin'"—Jay-Z

(Continued)

Name	Birth Year	Years of Experience in 2012	School Location (US)	School Type	Current Grade and Subject	Favorite HipHop Songs
Karlton Lattimer	1970	18 years	South East—large urban city	Public elementary	Fifth—math	"Thug Passion"—Tupac
Jovan Browne	1977	7 years	Mid-Atlantic—small suburban town	Christian K–8	Fourth; fifth; sixth; seventh; eighth—science	"Be a Father to Your Child"—Ed O.G. & Da Bulldogs *Midnight Marauders*—A Tribe Called Quest
Cole Boyd	1988	2 years	South East—small suburban town	Public elementary	Second—all subjects	"A Milli"—Lil Wayne "Successful"—Drake
Morris Bowman	1984	5 years	South East—small suburban town	Public elementary	Fifth—language arts and science (single gender)	"Justify My Thug" & "Heart of the City"—Jay-Z "Keep Your Head Up"—Tupac "Dear Mama"—Tupac "Black on Both Sides"—Mos Def

Appendix C
Answering My Research Questions

Question 1: What Are the Types of Life Experiences That Shape Black Men From the HipHop Generation Into Elementary School Teachers?

I have confirmed Dr. Marvin Lynn's declaration that Black boys need to see walking counternarratives in the elementary school classroom.[92] They need to see what is possible.[93] Black boys need to see that they are smart and important enough to not just graduate from high school, but that they are also smart and important enough to graduate from college and compete within the professional academic world. My findings demonstrate that Black men from the HipHop generation also need to have people in their lives who have high expectations and want to see them succeed. The men in this study had mentors in the form of teachers, coaches, neighborhood business owners, and upperclassmen who took the time from their daily lives to listen to and determine what their mentees' needs were, and then took the time to do something about it. For many of these men, this support came in the form of an otherfather[94] named HipHop.

Their lives were filled with teachers who cared enough about them to go above and beyond the call of duty, like when one gentleman's teacher gave him the opportunity to raise money to pay for class field trips (Morris Bowman). Effective, supportive teachers are one of the most common, important factors in Black boys' decision to become teachers themselves.[95] The participants' lives were also filled with coaches who took a vested interest in seeing them succeed—not just in the sport—but in life.[96] These coaches helped these young men by providing religious and spiritual guidance (Rob Porter), took care of them by taking them out to dinner (Victor Lucas), and taught them how to find the confidence within and to believe in themselves (Karlton Lattimer). Their lives were filled with neighborhood business owners who took a chance on them when they had no skills or prior experience—only the drive and desire to work (Morris Bowman). Their lives were filled with knowledgeable upperclassmen who took the time from their studies to sit and talk to open-minded freshmen about diversifying America's classrooms (Morris Bowman, Cole Boyd). The gentlemen in this study had the experience of mentorship in their lives and experienced encouragement and praise. Several of them had people in their lives who picked them up and brushed off their shoulders and told them they could do it. In conclusion, these are the types of life experiences that shape Black men from the HipHop generation into elementary school teachers.

Question 2: What Inspires Black Men to Teach Elementary School Children Despite the Societal Stigmas?

There were so many factors that inspired these men to choose this career path. They were not swayed by the meager salaries or low social status. Neither were they swayed by the stigma that may come with being mislabeled as homosexual or as a pedophile. In fact, several of them (Shawn Wise, Rob Porter, Caleb Mitchell) had devised crafty investment strategies to supplement their salaries and also expressed enough of a cool confidence and strong sense of self to diminish any concern about what others might imagine their "social status" or sexual orientation to be. The gentlemen in this study teach elementary school in spite of the societal stigmas that still plague our society. They teach despite the alienation they sometimes experience in what some deem a "women's profession." They teach because they want to disrupt negative images of men in the media and destroy stereotypes that men do not have, what some call, the *maternal instincts* to be effective teachers.[97] They teach because they care about children and because they enjoy working with children. They teach because they want to help young Black boys be successful in a world that does not always love or understand them.

Because African American male students have limited experiences with African American men teachers who may possess unique cultural and gendered perspectives that their woman-identified counterparts lack,[98] the gentlemen in this study seek to fill that void. They teach because they want to change the face of America's classrooms (Cole Boyd, Morris Bowman). They are inspired to teach because someone helped them, and they want to pay that support forward (Caleb Mitchell, Shawn Wise). They are inspired by the teachers who helped them outside of the classroom, by acknowledging their socioeconomic status without highlighting it or using it as a tool to embarrass them (Victor Lucas). They felt inspired because they did not feel fulfilled in the careers in which they were working (Karlton Lattimer, Jovan Browne). They were inspired by family members who led by example (Rob Porter, Jovan Browne, Cole Boyd). They had family members who were principals, teachers, and college professors; they had college-educated parents and family members who pushed and encouraged them to do well in school (Benjamin Robinson, Caleb Mitchell, Victor Lucas, Rob Porter, Jovan Browne). They were inspired by life changes. They were inspired by God.

They were inspired by the children. They were inspired by the love and open-hearted eagerness for learning that the children displayed and their passion for working with those children (Shawn Wise, Karlton Lattimer, Jovan Browne). They were inspired by their successful interactions with young people as they performed community service. They were inspired during their student teaching experiences (Morris Bowman, Cole Boyd, Caleb Mitchell). They were inspired because they could relate to many of the struggles of the children with whom they had experiences.[99] They were inspired to specifically teach on the elementary level because they enjoyed working within a broader context (teaching all subjects and life skills) instead of just one subject. Though I found the sources of inspiration to be quite varied, sources included positive experiences with mentors and other significant adults in their lives as well as with youth in nonacademic environments (Big Brother programs, after-school programs, etc.)

Question 3: How Does HipHop Culture Impact the Identity Development and Pedagogy of Black Men Who Become Elementary School Teachers?

The Black men in this study were all born between 1965 and 1988 and are, hence, considered to be a part of the HipHop generation. This era, especially for Black youth can be defined by the music, dress, language, world perspective, business acumen, and art that have come to be known as HipHop culture. HipHop encouraged them to think in innovative ways. Like me, many of the men in this study have been undercover critical race theorists. I say this because, like me, they recognized and critiqued the centrality of race and racism in their daily lives. This is part of the reason they cling to HipHop in such a prolific manner. HipHop encouraged them to look beyond the obvious, to look beyond what the majority told them to be true, and to step out and take risks. It opened their eyes to what was going on in the world and helped them to express themselves, feeling validated for just being Black men.

The Black men in this study not only understand the conscious-raising spirit of "old school HipHop," but they also appreciate the money-chasing souls of contemporary HipHop. The HipHop music that played while they were growing up inspired them to be self-educated. It inspired them to strive for better lives. It inspired them to fight against oppression. HipHop has served as a sort of otherfather to these men as it has mentored and guided them in how to approach manhood. They were immersed in HipHop culture, so as they grew and were impacted by other forces (family, educators, friends, community members), something inside guided them into the elementary school classroom. I do not claim that "HipHop made them do it." However, I do believe that the consciousness-raising aspect of HipHop has helped them to open their eyes and critically view the world around them. The gentlemen in this study represent the perpetuation of the Black freedom struggle as they use HipHop to help their students' quest for self-determination and a liberatory educative experience. Seeing the social hierarchy and the sorting and stratification processes happening in schools (and being victims of it themselves), these men became aware—at various points in their lives—that they needed to be a part of the change. They witnessed the evolution of HipHop. They observed HipHop as it grew and changed, so they had proof that change was possible.

Because these men grew up immersed in HipHop culture, they brought their own personal histories with them to their elementary classrooms. For them, HipHop is not just a music; it is a culture. It is all around them. It is all over them. They embody it. They wear it. They talk it. They walk it. Therefore, it is only appropriate that it would be prevalent in their pedagogy. They utilize HipHop cultural tendencies to connect with and relate to their students. Critical race praxis is prevalent in the stories the gentlemen in the study shared with me. They utilize HipHop to challenge dominant ideologies. They use HipHop because they respect counter-storytelling. They utilize the music of HipHop to help students make authentic connections to subject matter. They utilize HipHop as a form of critical pedagogy to help students see beyond the obvious and learn about the world in ways that help the students expand their thinking and become critical consumers in a world that is thoroughly obsessed with the commodification of the Black male body, especially as it relates to HipHop music and culture.

Appendix D
Looking Ahead: Implications for Future Research for Researchers

I have had the humble pleasure to meet and interact with nine amazing Black men who were born during the HipHop generation and serve elementary school children across this country as their teachers. Having heard, interpreted, analyzed, and shared their stories, I know there is still much to learn about Black men elementary school teachers from the HipHop generation. First, a qualitative study on Black men elementary teachers from the HipHop generation has serious implications for teacher education programs and school districts interested in balancing the gender and racial diversity in America's elementary level classrooms. I identified five of the purposes for teaching that drive the participants and their correlating chapters:

- Teaching as an act of resistance ("I Decide What a Black Man is Every Day")
- Teaching as an act of otherfathering ("Whose World in This?")
- Teaching as a calling ("The Elementary School was Where I Needed to Be")
- Teaching as an act of passion ("I Can't Hug the Kids")
- Teaching as an expression of HipHop ("The Solution Has to Be a Collective Effort")

Interested teacher education programs and school districts can utilize this information to help recruit, train, and retain Black men teachers by designing programs that provide training in liberatory educative experiences such as Critical HipHop Pedagogy. Also, by taking the time to learn more about what Black men are passionate about, by speaking to these passions, and providing a supportive place that encourages them to follow their innermost passions (without fear of vilification), interested agencies might be able to see an increase in the quantity of Black men who more willingly and readily decide to join the ranks of the elementary teaching force. Furthermore, it is essential for teacher education programs to know that three of the nine men who participated in this study chose to become *elementary education* majors based on their student teaching experiences and/or discussions with their academic advisors. Hence, I deduce that student teaching and advisement had a profound impact on which grade levels the gentlemen in this study decided to teach as well.

Second, more research is needed to unpack the impact of coaching on teaching as it pertains to all educational stakeholders, especially Black men teachers and students. Several of the gentlemen spoke passionately about their coaches and the impact that they had on their lives inside and outside of school. There are programs such as the Promoting Academic Achievement through Sports (PASS)[100] that assists teachers in making use of some of the practical instructional strategies used in coaching to help improve academic success.[101] Jeffrey Duncan-Andrade delves deeply into this topic in his 2010 book *What a Coach Can Teach a Teacher*. So there is already a ready section of literature on this topic. Therefore, someone looking to explore this research topic has a firm place to start.

Next, I feel that research is needed to explore the impact that Black men elementary school teachers have on Black girls and children of different racial backgrounds. The concept of fatherloss can affect all children, and girls feel the effects of fatherloss as well as boys do. How this translates into the dearth of Black men teachers would be an interesting point of study. In my full study, I briefly discuss how Black girls from the HipHop generation were impacted by fatherloss, and several of the participants in this study shared that they feel their presence impacts girls in a positive way as well. Furthermore, they also shared that they felt that their presence impacted a diverse range of children (races and genders). Research is needed to determine the effects of Black men elementary school teachers on children of all racial backgrounds. How does their presence, and the interesting perspectives that men from this particular generation bring to the classroom, impact all children? This is an area that warrants further exploration and discussion.

Also, there is a beautiful knowledge base that defines and illuminates characteristics of the "HipHop generation"—who we are, what we do, and how we behave. However, HipHop is a culture that is continuing to grow as the decades pass and to expand its reach across the globe. HipHop is now 50 years old and spans the entirety of two+ generations. Thus, I see the potential for research on the second and third HipHop generations. How are those people born from 1985 to 2004 different than those of us born between 1965 and 1984? How are those folk born from 2005 to 2023 different from the first two generations? How are we the same? As HipHop is a dynamic culture that has changed and evolved since its inception, what characteristics might a second and third HipHop generation (one that was raised on Lil Wayne, Wiz Khalifa, Megan Thee Stallion, Lil Uzi Vert, and Latto) have that sets them apart from the other generations? How might they change the world?

My last suggestion for future research involves the intentional, systemic integration of HipHop culture into curriculum. There is a thriving cadre of scholarship on HipHop pedagogy by scholars such as A.A. Akom, David Stovall, Bettina L. Love, Marc Lamont Hill. However, more research is needed to study how this particular population, Black men born during the HipHop generation who teach elementary school, utilize HipHop in their daily practice. Still, not much is known about Black men elementary school teachers, but their voices deserve consistently continued amplification.

Appendix E
Resources for Black Men Teachers[102]

The following alphabetical list of resources has been gathered through research and personal connections. Please note that not all have been vetted. Though I have had the honor of working directly with several of the programs listed below, please do further research before divulging any personal information or giving too much of your time or energy to any program, agency, or organization. This is not an exhaustive list, and in my human walk, I am sure that I have omitted many other incredibly important and empowering programs. Please use this list as a starting point for you on your journey. I pray you find what you need.

AFRICAN AMERICAN MALE TEACHER INITIATIVE

Website: https://htu.edu/academics/colleges/cas/dept-of-educator-preparation/african-american-male-teacher-initiative

The Apple Pre-Ed Scholars Program, housed within Huston-Tillotson University's 100 African American Male Teacher Initiative funded by Apple Inc., provides 1 year of scholarship support to high-achieving Huston-Tillotson freshmen who intend to pursue a career in Education. Teaching career fields include the following majors: English, History, Kinesiology, Mathematics, Music, and Science with an Education minor. Scholars are selected on the basis of financial need, academic performance, demonstration of leadership, commitment to service, and dedication to pursuing a career in the Education field. Total award will cover all tuition, fees, room, and board for an academic year. Scholarships are eligible for a maximum 3-year renewal, depending on meeting scholarship requirements, persistence toward graduation, demonstrated financial need, and availability of funding.

BLACK MALE EDUCATORS ALLIANCE (BMEA)

Website: https://blackmaleeducatorsalliance.org/

Black Male Educators Alliance (BMEA) is a 501(c)(3) nonprofit founded in 2017 with an original targeted focus on increasing the percentage of Black males in the classroom in the State of Michigan. Since then, BMEA's vision has evolved to liberating students, teachers, school leaders, and school systems/policies to transform the landscape of education for Black and Brown communities across the country. BMEA works with educators and schools in Michigan, Illinois, New York, Ohio, and China.

- Mission:
  - We exist to transform the school experience for Black and Brown children by creating culturally sustaining policies, structured programming, and teacher pedagogy that develops students into change agents for their community.
- Vision:
  - BMEA is dedicated to liberating students, teachers, school leaders, and school systems/policies to transform the landscape of education for Black and Brown communities across the country.
- Core Values
  - Integrity
  - Love and care
  - Commitment
  - Execution

BLACK MEN TEACH

Website: https://blackmenteachtc.org/

From recruitment, to helping select the appropriate training program, to securing resources to assist in paying for that training, to placement in schools that have strong induction programs, career growth opportunities, and supportive cultures, Black Men Teach supports the growth of Black male educators in Twin Cities schools. From the moment a man indicates that he wants to be a teacher, we will help him navigate the process and show him a pathway to success.

- Mission:
  - To recruit, prepare, place, and retain Black male teachers in elementary schools.
- Vision:
  - All students have the opportunity to attend schools staffed with racially and culturally diverse teachers and leaders, reflecting the students' race, ethnicity and cultures, thereby creating an environment that affirms students for whom they are.
- Goals:
  - Black Men Teach creates the environment and conditions where Black male teachers can thrive, because our children's schooling experience will never be complete without them. Black Men Teach addresses all the challenges faced by Black male teacher candidates.
    - Recruitment
    - Training options and cost
    - Induction
    - School culture
    - Meaningful career paths
    - Adequate compensation

BROTHERS EMPOWERED TO TEACH

Website: https://www.be2t.org/

- Mission:
  - We provide mentorship, apprenticeship, and pathways to careers in education through early exposure to teaching and targeted experiences cultivating an organic love of teaching children.
- Vision:
  - Brothers Empowered to Teach (BE2T) envisions a world where every child can see themselves in and through the eyes of their teacher.
- Core Values:
  - Remain relevant
    - It is important that our fellows understand the language, likes, dislikes, and social issues affecting the students in their

classrooms. It is equally important that BE2T understands the issues and the trends that affect our fellows. From our vantage point, having the ability to create pathways to open dialogue is the key to building cultural competency in a holistic way.

- Be comfortable with being uncomfortable
  - Growth requires one to stretch beyond comfort zones. We challenge ourselves throughout the entire program to look for ways to improve how we do our work. To achieve our goals, we may reach places which require us to learn from the struggle and embrace it.
- Always be prepared for game day
  - Ninety percent of success is preparation. We want to be ready to seize opportunities for others. Preparation plus the ability to relate, communicate, and present our best selves widens our access and ability to grow.
- Hustle With Grit
  - Nothing beats failure but a try. In that, there is no failure … only lessons. Developing BE2T has not come without its share of losses. These losses have helped us gain clarity on what we want to accomplish. We are accessible examples of how to continue to climb even in challenging times for those who participate in our program.
- Take care (social and emotional self-care)
  - BE2T wants to support the development of each of our participants in a holistic way. The foundation to this development is taking care of oneself emotionally. By promoting social and emotional awareness, our participants will have the foundation to better manage the stressors as a teacher and as simply a human being.
- Defy convention
  - Popular opinion says Black men don't teach, and the statistics support that. Only two percent of all teachers nationally are Black men. We want our fellows to turn the profession on its head by entering the classroom and using their ability to communicate and relate to the students they teach every day. We meet teachers every day who demonstrate that Black men can and do teach. We have to show more Black men that regardless of what the masses say, they have the ability to reach at-risk students that defies the current demographic

in front of the classroom and the vision of what success looks like to students.

BMESTALK

Website: https://bmestalk.com/

BMEsTalk was founded to ensure that BMEs have a culturally affirming professional learning community and leadership tools that inspires them to continue positively impacting the lives of all students, particularly Black boys, in schools. BMEsTalk serves Black men working across district, charter, independent, parochial, and international TK–12 schools.

- Mission
  - To create and curate safe, rich spaces for BMEs to connect, grow, and lead.
- Vision
  - To inspire Black Male Educators (BMEs) to achieve their full potential.
- Leadership Development Programs
  - Catalyst:
    - The BMEsTalk Catalyst is a 4-day in-person, experiential, and inspirational leadership development workshop. Taking place in Atlanta, GA, over the summer. Black men educators will join a diverse cohort of leaders who are other Black men advancing in their careers, possessing a wealth of expertise, cultural knowledge, and lived experiences.
  - Incubator:

    The BMEsTalk Incubator is a 10-month facilitative leadership certification program. Join the Incubator to build connections that last a lifetime; land your dream job; increase your annual income. Our Incubator is a thoughtfully curated leader and leadership development journey that will equip you with the tools, knowledge, and personalized community of support you need to transform the way you lead leaders.
  - Leadership Lab:
    - The BMEsTalk Leadership Lab is a series of four virtual affinity group convenings curated for and by BMEs. Each

convening is experiential, offering you the space to be heard, feel energized, and inspire other men that look like you.

CALL ME MISTER

Website: https://www.clemson.edu/education/programs/programs/call-me-mister.html

The Call Me MISTER® program is contributing to the talent pool of excellent teachers by identifying and supporting students such as Mr. Mark Joseph who are literally "touching the future" by teaching children. Mark's teaching degree was made possible through the Call Me MISTER® program. Call Me MISTER® was developed by some of our State's visionary educational leaders who sincerely believe we can build a better tomorrow by getting you involved today.

- Mission:
    - The mission of the Call Me MISTER® (acronym for Mentors Instructing Students Toward Effective Role Models) Initiative is to increase the pool of available teachers from a broader more diverse background particularly among the State's lowest performing elementary schools. Student participants are largely selected from among underserved, socioeconomically disadvantaged, and educationally at-risk communities.

- Program Benefits:
    - The project provides:
        - Tuition assistance through Loan Forgiveness programs for admitted students pursuing approved programs of study in teacher education at participating colleges.
        - An academic support system to help assure their success.
        - A cohort system for social and cultural support.
        - Assistance with job placement.

CENTER FOR RESEARCH & MENTORING OF BLACK MALE STUDENTS & TEACHERS

Website: https://bowiestate.edu/academics/colleges/college-of-education/special-projects/center-for-black-males/

The Center at Bowie State University seeks to support a pipeline of Black males who want to enter the education profession, where Black males only represent 2 percent of teachers in US public schools.

- Mission:
  - To provide expertise on matters about Black male students and teachers in Maryland and throughout the nation by disseminating information, providing innovative programming, securing funding, and working with partners and stakeholders.
- Vision:
  - To be a premier national leader, clearinghouse, and model for research and scholarship, evaluation, mentorship, policies, theory, professional development, best practices, and services for Black male students and teachers.
- Objectives:
  - To achieve the vision and mission, the center staff will work to:
    - Create a space for Black boys and men to feel safe, be themselves, supported, connected, and have a community committed to ensuring their success academically, socially, professionally, entrepreneurially, or whatever they decide to do.
    - Produce quality research and scholarship on Black male students and teachers.
    - Publish articles, book chapters, reports, evaluations, policy papers, journal special issues, and books focused on Black male students and teachers.
    - Pursue and secure internal and external funding to support the center vision and mission.
    - Provide innovative programming to Black male students and teachers.
    - Provide an innovative program to families of Black male students and prospective Black male teachers.
    - Provide research opportunities to undergraduate, masters, and doctoral students interested in serving Black male students and teachers and their families.
    - Provide consultation and professional development to leaders, teachers, individual schools, school districts, educational organizations, colleges/universities, mentoring organizations, and other institutions on matters related to Black male students and teachers.

- Identify and apply best practices for recruiting, retaining, and supporting Black male teachers across the educational and professional trajectory.
- Identify and apply practices for achieving the best academic and social development of Black male students throughout the prekindergarten to doctoral educational journey.
- Advise government officials and policymakers on designing effective policies and services for Black male students and teachers.

HE IS ME INSTITUTE

Website: https://heisme.org/

- Mission:
  - He is Me Institute ensures that Black male teachers have lifelong access to resources, experiences, and opportunities that support them as they are recruited, retained, and retire as teachers.
- Vision:
  - We envision a society in which racial wealth inequity is obsolete and where all students have the academic experience of learning from teachers of all backgrounds, especially Black men. After learning from a diverse group of instructors, children grow up better educated. As a result, they gain more access to resources & opportunities that create generational wealth and enjoy a better quality of life.
- Our Values:
  - *Lead* with empathy
  - *Act* with integrity
  - *Experience* growth through struggle
  - *Learn* through reflection

LEADING MEN FELLOWSHIP

Website: https://theliteracylab.org/leading-men/

The Literacy Lab's Leading Men Fellowship creates opportunities for young men of color and increases representation in the field of education.

Leading Men Fellows are young men of color who have recently graduated from high school and participate in a year-long, residency-style experience in which they provide evidence-based literacy support to prekindergarten students while receiving robust coaching and professional development and gaining valuable experience.

- Mission:
    - The Literacy Lab provides students—in communities experiencing racial and/or economic inequities—with evidence-based, culturally responsive literacy instruction as preparation for academic, professional, and personal success.
    - The Literacy Lab serves children from age three through grade three. We partner with school districts to help close the literacy gap largely by embedding full-time, rigorously trained tutors in early childhood centers and elementary schools.
- Vision:
    - We believe literacy is a human right. When we achieve our mission, we will have created a more just society where all students have the literacy services needed to unlock educational opportunities and success in life.

NATIONAL ASSOCIATION OF BLACK MALE EDUCATORS

Website: https://nabme.org/

- Mission:
    - The mission of the National Association of Black Male Educators is to dramatically increase the number of marginalized children who succeed by dramatically increasing the number of highly effective Black and Brown male teachers and leaders who positively impact them.
- Vision:
    - By 2035, the National Association of Black Male Educators will be widely known for creating:
        - An abundance of classically trained Black and Brown men who have secured positions in education.

- An abundance of highly effective Black and Brown male leaders leading high-performing schools and school districts across the nation.
- An emerging cadre of Black and Brown male high-school students entering college with a focus on education and the goal of becoming educators.
- An abundance of educated and knowledgeable Black and Brown men directly impacting the shifts in policies within education needed to ensure equity for all children.
- An abundance of influential Black and Brown male educational leaders directly contributing to the success and achievement of Black and Brown men in education, closing the equity and achievement gap for marginalized children.

PROFOUND GENTLEMEN

Website: https://www.profoundgentlemen.org/

- Mission:
  - Our mission is to build a community of male Educators of Color who provide a profound additional impact on boys of color. We develop, support, and retain highly effective male teachers of color across the nation to positively affect the academic achievement of all children in traditional public and charter schools, with particular attention to the achievement of boys of color.
- Values:
  - Our History and Core Values Keep Us Rooted in the Work.
    - **Love:** We love one another through our actions and character. Love is the respect we give to ourselves and others. Love is how we approach our work.
    - **Authenticity:** We bring our most authentic selves into spaces. Authenticity is the vulnerability we bring to PG's inclusive spaces. Vulnerability is encouraged but never forced; however, we are excited to find opportunities to share our stories and pivotal moments that shaped who we are today.
    - **Unity:** We find opportunities to collaborate with our community. We cultivate opportunities to support each other, leveraging our staff, educators, and community members' unique abilities to make a collective impact on the communities they

support. The PG space is open to everyone regardless of race, gender, sexual orientation, culture, or religion.
- **Growth Mindset:** We think differently. We embrace opportunities to learn from our success and failures and remain committed to a continuous learning process in our vision.
- **Hope:** We are optimistic in our approach to this work. While challenging at times, we still find joy in the small moments and work to improve the outcomes of our communities regardless of the obstacles that arise.
- **Servant Leadership:** We lead with humility and do what's necessary for the advancement of our communities. We recognize that the betterment of our communities requires us to remain rooted in the community and propel us forward. We seek ways to leverage our past, knowledge, and skills to progress the movement.

SUMMER HOUSE INSTITUTE

Website: https://www.summerhouseco.org/

- Mission:
  - At Summer House, we take research-backed approaches and innovate on new ways to apply them to achieve greater equity. We provide pathways into the work through tailored early exposure and preservice support opportunities. Our program builds skills in an affinity-based community of inclusion. Our theory of change positions Summer House as a "gateway" organization working with Fellows from the start of their college career experience and partnering with them to support their professional pathway. Summer House is a catalyst into the education career field by providing a tight community, tailored curriculum, and introductions to seasoned professionals and mentors. Our affinity-based approach increases participants' confidence and sense of belonging in the field. Upon completing the fellowship, the cohort will graduate college with a clear career trajectory.
- Vision:
  - The fully realized vision of Summer House will be the legacy that Black men are assets to the community in which they live. Our explicit goal is to have 1500 Black men added to schools due to our program by 2030. To help achieve this goal, we must expand

into chapter cities to broaden our reach. We are poised to deliver a cohort of 25 Black male college students across our chapter cities every year to become teachers in our partnering school districts. When schools are more reflective of the communities they serve, research shows the confidence of parents, students, and the community increases.

- Program Pillars
  - Listen + Learn
    - Participants will hear from top thinkers, practitioners, and leaders in the space to better understand the role of leadership and how to approach the work and world of Public Education.
  - Observe + Act
    - Throughout the Observe and Act sessions, SHI CMs will have the opportunity to observe leaders from the Listen and Learn sections in their day-to-day practices.
  - PD Sessions
    - Participants will be exposed to interactive PD lessons from SHI Leaders so that they can learn and grow in knowledge. Cohort members will then be prompted to reflect upon their learnings from the prior week to demonstrate mastery of new content.
  - Capstone
    - The capstone project for the SHI's cohort will be focused on lifting up and empowering each CM through podcasting. Throughout the summer, CMs will learn the basics of recording, producing, and editing their own podcast episode.

THE BOND PROJECT

Website: https://bondeducators.org/

The Building Our Network of Diversity (BOND) Project is committed to advancing efforts to recruit, develop, support, and retain male educators of color. The BOND Project demonstrates its commitment through professional enrichment, mentoring, scholarship, and fellowship activities for educators across the country.

- Goals:
  - Recruitment
    - To advocate for increased hiring of male educators of color
  - Development
    - To increase educator capacity via professional development, presentations, and scholarships
  - Retention
    - To serve as a mentoring network for male educators of color that provides support and understanding of professional advancement and retention processes
  - Empowerment
    - To promote student and educator agency to disrupt systemic inequities and advocate for equitable access to educational opportunities

CENTER FOR BLACK EDUCATOR DEVELOPMENT

Website: https://www.thecenterblacked.org/bmec

The Center for Black Educator Development recognizes that supporting and uplifting BMEs is integral to transforming the education sector for the better. Black Men in Education Convening (BMEC) is one approach we're taking to recruit, support, retain, and activate more Black men to revolutionize the educational system.

- Mission:
  - To ensure there will be equity in the recruiting, training, hiring, and retention of quality educators that reflect the cultural background and share common sociopolitical interests of the students they serve.
- Vision:
  - All Black students will have consistent access to high quality, same race teachers throughout their Pre-K–12 experience.
  - Teachers who do not share the same cultural backgrounds as their students will demonstrate high levels of expertise in culturally responsive practices and anti-discriminatory mindsets and habits.

- Professional learning, pipeline, policies, and pedagogy will be aligned to ensure greater educator diversity, cultural responsiveness, and improved student outcomes.

THE TEACHERS' LOUNGE[103]

Website: https://theteachersloungema.org/

The Teachers' Lounge seeks to drive unprecedented student outcomes by greatly diversifying the people, thoughts, and actions of the educational workforce in the Greater Boston Area and beyond.

- Mission:
  - In efforts to recruit, revitalize, and retain Educators of Color, The Teachers' Lounge develops and implements innovative solutions for building more diverse, equitable, and inclusive learning and professional environments for all stakeholders.
- Vision:
  - The Teachers' Lounge is an education-based nonprofit organization seeking to drive unprecedented student outcomes by greatly diversifying the people, thoughts, and actions of the educational workforce in the Greater Boston Area and beyond.
- Programming
  - Community cultivation
    - Educators of Color from across the Commonwealth join a community that affirms the rich diversity of experiences and backgrounds rarely reflected in our schools, at present.
  - Learning and development
    - Educators of Color take part in our monthly panels, workshops, and professional development programming to improve individual and collective practice. Schools, organizations, and community partners are supported in developing and implementing equity-centered hiring and retention strategies.
  - Sustainability and growth
    - Through our Classroom Leaders of Color (CLOC) Fellowship, we seek to provide continued support, coaching,

mentorship, and resources to address the specific needs of early career Educators of Color, therefore improving the skills, well-being, and sustainability of cohort members.

- Representative research
  - We engage in research, analysis, consultation, and synthesis of information, rooted in the lived experiences of Educators of Color, to produce thoughts, ideas, and practical approaches to promoting equity in our education system in an attempt to build stronger recruitment pipelines and retention strategies for Educators of Color.
- Career advancement and mobility
  - Educators of Color are connected with other Educators of Color and Hiring Managers from our 191 school/district partners to gain access to new resources and opportunities. Hiring Managers are connected to a diverse collective of Educators of Color across 10 months of TTL programming, allowing opportunities to develop sustainable relationships. Candidates and hiring managers gain access to a job portal and virtual hiring fair, where Educators of Color are in the driver's seat of the career exploration experience.

Notes

1. Dr. Daniella A. Cook thoroughly and beautifully describes the process of "writing CRT" in Cook, D. A., "Blurring the Boundaries: The Mechanics of Creating Composite Characters," in *Handbook of Critical Race Theory in Education*, eds M. Lynn and A. D. Dixson (New York: Routledge, 2013), 181–94.
2. Bell, Derrick, "Who's Afraid of Critical Race Theory?" *University of Illinois Law Review* 1995, no. 4 (1995): 893–910.
3. The Kikuyu people, also called Gikuyu or Agikuyu, are Bantu-speaking people who live in the highland area of south-central Kenya, near Mount Kenya. https://www.britannica.com/topic/Kikuyu.
4. SoHo is the commonly used abbreviation for South of Houston Street.
5. Morgan, Joan, When Chickenheads Come Home To Roost: A Hip-Hop Feminist Breaks It Down (New York: Simon and Schuster, 2017).
6. Matias, Cheryl E., "'Mommy, Is Being Brown Bad?': Critical Race Parenting in a 'Post-Race' Era." *Journal of Race and Pedagogy* 1, no. 3 (2016): 12. Article 1. http://soundideas.pugetsound.edu/rpj/vol1/iss3/1
7. The "City" is the common colloquialism that New Yorkers use when referencing Manhattan, or New York City.
8. hooks, bell, *Sisters of the Yam: Black Women and Self-Recovery* (Boston, MA: South End Press, 1993), 1.
9. Phillips, Stephanie L., "Beyond Competitive Victimhood: Abandoning Arguments that Black Women or Black Men Are Worse Off," in *Progressive Black Masculinities?* ed. Stephanie L. Phillips (London: Routledge, 2006), 223.

10. Shange, Ntozake, For Colored Girls Who Have Considered Suicide/When the Rainbow is Enuf (New York: Scribner, 1989), 261.
11. Kuumba, M. Bahati, "Gender Justice: Linking Women's Human Rights and Progressive Black Masculinities," in *Progressive Black Masculinities*, ed. A. D. Mutua (New York: Routledge, 2006), 238.
12. According to Crenshaw, Kimberlé, Neil Gotanda, Gary Peller, and Kendall Thomas, eds, *Critical Race Theory: The Key Writings That Formed the Movement* (New York: The New Press, 1995), the term Critical Race Theory was coined in 1989 by Kimberle Crenshaw, Neil Gotanda, and Stephanie "to make it clear that our work locates itself in intersection of critical theory and race, racism and the law" (p. xxvii).
13. Solórzano, D. G., and T. Yosso, "Critical Race Methodology: Counter-Storytelling as an Analytical Framework for Education Research," *Qualitative Inquiry* 23–44 (2002): 25.
14. Bell, "Who's Afraid of Critical Race Theory?"
15. Tafari, Dawn N. Hicks, "'Whose World is This?': A Composite Counterstory of Black Male Elementary School Teachers as Hip-Hop Otherfathers," *The Urban Review: Issues and Ideas in Public Education* (2018): 795–817.
16. Tafari, Dawn N. Hicks, "I Can't Hug the Kids: A Composite Counterstory of Black Men Elementary School Teachers Who Love What They Do," in *Intersectionality of Race, Class, and Gender with Teaching and Teacher Education: Movement Toward Equity in Education*, ed. N. P. Carter (Danvers, MA: Brill—Sense, 2018), 99–109.
17. Bell, Derrick, Faces at the Bottom of the Well: The Permanence of Racism (New York: Basic Books, 1992).
18. Cook, "Blurring the Boundaries."
19. Cook, D. A., and A. D. Dixson, "Writing Critical Race Theory and Method: A Composite Counterstory on the Experiences of Black Teachers in New Orleans Post-Katrina," *International Journal of Qualitative Studies in Education* 26, no. 10 (2013): 1238–58.
20. Solórzano and Yosso, "Critical Race Methodology."
21. Cook, "Blurring the Boundaries."
22. Solórzano and Yosso, "Critical Race Methodology," 36.

23. Solórzano Daniel, and Tara J. Yosso helped me to frame my analysis of the men's stories by illustrating the functions that counterstories serve: "(a) They can build community among those at the margins of society by putting a human and familiar face to educational theory and practice, (b) they can challenge the perceived wisdom of those at society's center by providing a context to understand and transform established belief systems, (c) they can open new windows into the reality of those at the margins of society by showing possibilities beyond the ones they live and demonstrating that they are not alone in their position, and (d) they can teach others that by combining elements from both the story and the current reality, one can construct another world that is richer than either the story or the reality alone" (2002: 36).
24. Here I quote rapper, Milk Dee, from the HipHop group Audio Two. The referenced line is from the song "Top Billin'" on the album, *What More Can I Say?*, which was released in 1988.
25. "Lyte As a Rock" is the title of a rap song released in 1988 by HipHop artist MC Lyte. The song plays on the oxymoronic simile, light as a rock, to give credit to "how heavy the young lady is." A trailblazer, MC Lyte was the first solo female rap artist to release a full album (*Lyte As a Rock*, 1988). Today, she is still one of my favorite artists.
26. The terms "sista" and "sister" used here both represent the relationship Kamau has with these two women. Dawn is a "sista" because she is a Black woman, significant of a sort of fictive kinship held among Black folk. The term "sister" speaks to Kamau's biological sister.
27. The song "Big Pimpin'," by HipHop artist, Jay Z, was released in 2000 on his album *Vol. 3 ... Life and Times of S. Carter*. Southern HipHop duo UGK are featured on this song.
28. In *The Hip Hop Generation: Young Blacks and the Crisis in African American Culture* (2002), Bakara Kitwana defined the HipHop Generation as Black people born between 1965 and 1984 and as a generation that "birthed itself."
29. "The Message" was released in 1982 by Grandmaster Flash and the Furious Five on their album, *The Message*.
30. "The Corner" was released in 2005 by Common, featuring Kanye West and The Last Poets, for Common's album, *Be*.

31. HBCU is the common abbreviation for Historically Black College and University.
32. This research on high-school graduation and dropout rates, special education and suspension referrals, and achievement data is specially supported by the following sources: Ann Arnett Ferguson's 2001 text *Bad Boys: Public Schools in The Making of Black Masculinity*; Charles P. Gause's 2008 text *Integration Matters: Navigating Identity, Culture, and Resistance;* Jawanza Kunjufu's 1985 text *Countering the Conspiracy to Destroy Black Boys*; Pedro A. Noguera's 2008 text *The Trouble With Black Boys .... And Other Reflections on Race, Equity, and the Future of Public Education;* and Alan Vanneman's July 2009 report, *Achievement Gaps: How Black and White Students in Public Schools Perform in Mathematics and Reading on the National Assessment of Educational Progress.*
33. Walking counter-narratives are Black men who demonstrate strength, beauty, and power and are positive examples of what Black boys are capable of achieving. Walking counter-narratives are described and defined in detail in Howard, T. C., "Reconceptualizing Multicultural Education: Design Principles for Educating African American Males," in *Black Sons to Mothers: Compliments. Critiques, and Challenges for Cultural Workers in Education*, eds. M. C. Brown II and J. E. Davis (New York: Peter Lang Publishing, Inc., 2000), 155–72 and Lynn, M., "Education for the Community: Exploring the Culturally Relevant Practices of Black Male Teachers," *Teachers College Record* 108, no. 12 (2006): 2497–522.
34. In her 1999 book, *When Chicken-Heads Come Home to Roost: A Hip-Hop Feminist Breaks It Down*, Joan Morgan coined the term HipHop Feminist and powerfully shifted the conversation about how Black women and Black men see the world, see one another, interact, and love.
35. Shange, N., "For Colored Girls Who Have Considered Suicide/When the Rainbow is Enuf," in P. C. Harrison, *Totem Voices: Plays from the Black World Repertory* (New York: Grove Press, 1989), 261.
36. The rap song "Back in the Day" was released in 1994 by HipHop artist, Ahmad. "Back in the Day" was the first single on Ahmad's self-titled first album, *Ahmad*.

37. A "pound" is an "urban" term used to describe a clasp of hands similar to a handshake.
38. The composite counterstory, Tafari, "I Can't Hug the Kids." Reprinted with permission.
39. Black Rob is the HipHop artist who performs "Star in Da Hood."
40. A. Phillip Randolph Campus High School is a 4-year public high school located in Manhattan, NY.
41. Translation: "Do you play ball here regularly?"
42. PSSA refers to the Pennsylvania System School Assessment, Pennsylvania's state-wide standardized test for children in grades 3–8. A proficient score indicates that the child has demonstrated "adequate" skills and is considered on grade level.
43. "I Need Love" was released by Def Jam Record in 1987. The song is performed by LL Cool J.
44. Another form of acknowledgment and/or form of affection, similar to a pound. "Dap" could be when one person taps the side of one fist on top of the side of the recipient's fist and vice versa; dap could be the same as a "pound."
45. The *Tamshi la Tambiko* is a libation prayer written by Dr. Maulana Karenga, the founder of Kwanzaa. This excerpt was borrowed from http://www.tupacshakurfoundation.org/events/kwanzaa/
46. On December 12, 2022, the Hill CDC (Hill Community Development Corporation) hosted a Pre-Kwanzaa Celebration at Nafasi on Centre (https://blackpittsburgh.com/pre-kwanzaa-celebration/). Please learn more about this important organization by visiting their website—https://www.hilldistrict.org/
47. The Pittsburgh Botanical Garden's Dazzling Nights experience was introduced in 2022. For more information, please visit https://www.discovertheburgh.com/christmas-lights-in-pittsburgh/
48. At the end of a Kwanzaa celebration, all attendees shout "*Harambee!*" seven times as the pull their upstretched fists down to their sides in unison. This phrase and action signify the closing of the Kwanzaa celebration. For more information about Kwanzaa, please visit https://www.officialkwanzaawebsite.org/index.html
49. The customary greeting during Kwanzaa is "*Habari Gani?*," which means "What's the news?" The recipient of the greeting responds

with the corresponding *Nguzo Saba* principle for the day. *Umoja* (Unity) is the first principle of the *Nguzo Saba* (seven principles).
50. This line is from the song titled, "Whoo Kid Freestyle," produced by DJ Whoo Kid and featuring G-Unit for 50 Cent's 2022 album *Guess Who's Back?*
51. Ibid.
52. "How to Rob" is a single on 50 Cent's 2000 album *Power of the Dollar*. The song was also featured on the *In Too Deep* (1999) movie soundtrack.
53. "Dear Mama" was the lead single from 2Pac's third studio album, *Me Against the World* released in 1995.
54. The composite counterstory "Whose World is This?" was originally published as part of a larger manuscript: Tafari, "Whose World is This?" Reprinted with permission.
55. The song being referenced and sung here is HipHop artist, Nas' song, "The World is Yours," released in 1994 on the album, *Illmatic*.
56. The song referenced here is Nas' "Queens Get the Money," released in 2008 on his *Untitled* album.
57. Kamau is referring to his school's Academically Gifted and Talented Program.
58. "You Must Learn" was recorded by Boogie Down Productions and released in 1989.
59. HipHop artist, KRS-One is also known as The Teacha because of his powerful rap style. He called his rhymes "edutainment" because his lyrics often included important facts about Black history. In addition, he made significant scholarly contributions to HipHop as a cultural institution, which can be seen in his books *KRS-One: Ruminations* (2003) and *The Gospel of Hip Hop: The First Instrument* (2009).
60. Written by Claude M. Steele (2011) *Whistling Vivaldi: How Stereotypes Affect Us and What We Can Do* is the seminal text on stereotype threat.
61. From Sargent, Paul. Real Men or Real Teachers? Contradictions in the lives of men elementary school teachers (Harriman, NY: Men's Studies Press, 2001), 61.
62. Ibid., 61–2.

63. Mr. Campbell is referencing the overall theme of the song "How to Rob" by 50 Cent.
64. This is the first line of the chorus in the song "How to Rob" by 50 Cent and the Mad Rapper. "How to Rob" is a single on 50 Cent's 2000 album *Power of the Dollar*. The song was also featured on the *In Too Deep* (1999) movie soundtrack.
65. A pseudonym is being used here to protect the identity of the participant.
66. Ibid.
67. Ibid.
68. "Fight the Power" was performed by the HipHop super group, Public Enemy and released as part of the *Do the Right Thing* soundtrack in 1988.
69. This phrase is from the song "Fight the Power."
70. "Sub" is a commonly used abbreviation among public school teachers for substitute teacher.
71. "We're here to serve children" is a phrase commonly used by Mr. Shaka Rawls, Principal of Leo Catholic School in Chicago, IL. Mr. Rawls is a prolific educator and administrator and a powerful speaker.
72. One of the most popular lyrics in "The Message," this line speaks to the overwhelming frustration felt from trying to navigate the often-tumultuous ebbs and flows of society. "The Message" was performed by Grandmaster Flash and The Furious Five and released in 1982 for the album *The Message*.
73. IPA is the abbreviation for India pale ale.
74. Published in 1999, *The Rose That Grew from Concrete* is a collection of poetry written by HipHop artist, Tupac Shakur.
75. The referenced line is the first line of the first verse of the Notorious B.I.G.'s song "Juicy," from his debut album, *Ready to Die* (1994).
76. ArtII.S1.C8.1 Oath of Office for the Presidency, https://constitution.congress.gov/browse/essay/artII-S1-C8-1/ALDE_00001126/
77. *Special* was released in 2022 and is the fourth studio album of the musical artist and musician Lizzo.
78. According to Britannica, misogyny, hatred, or prejudice against women, typically exhibited by men. It is generally accepted that

misogyny is a consequence of patriarchy (male-dominated society), and the term may be applied to certain individuals as well as larger systems, societies, or cultures. https://www.britannica.com/topic/misogyny

79. Merriam-Webster defines misogynoir as the hatred of, aversion to, or prejudice against Black women. https://www.merriam-webster.com/dictionary/misogynoir
80. "The Message" by Grandmaster Flash and the Furious Five was released in 1982 on the group's first studio album, *The Message*.
81. More information about these three agencies and other organizations that serve Black men teachers is provided in Appendix E.
82. hooks, bell, *We Real Cool: Black Men and Masculinity* (New York: Routledge, 2004), xii.
83. The concept of cerebral otherfathering is discussed on page 799 in Tafari, "Whose World is This?" Here, I used the term also to describe the impact bell hooks has had on my life.
84. I assigned pseudonyms to all study participants to protect their identity.
85. Doechii is a Black woman HipHop artist. She released "What It Is (Block Boy)" on March 17, 2023. The original version of the song features Kodak Black.
86. Fanon, F., *Black Skin, White Masks* (New York: Grove Press, 1967), 98.
87. Hickmon, J., B. Kapri, A. King, and B. Atterberry. 2023. "What It Is (Block Boy)"; Conds. J. White Did It and Kennedy; Comps. A. White, B. Kennedy, L. Edwards, J. Glaze, D. Prince, L. Jefferson, C. Love, J. Smith, K. Briggs, K. Burruss, T. Cottle, and M. Simmonds
88. See Solórzano and Yosso, 2002.
89. Spanish for "shit."
90. Bell, Faces at the Bottom of the Well: The Permanence of Racism.
91. In "Who Really Cares? The Disenfranchisement of African American Males in Pre-K-12 Schools: A Critical Race Theory Perspective." On pages 954–85 of *Teachers College Record* (2008), Tyrone C. Howard describes a critical race methodology as a "particular analytic lens [that] acknowledges the presence and perniciousness of racism, discrimination and hegemony, and enables various cultural and racial frames of reference to guide research questions, influence the methods

of collecting and analyzing data, and to inform how findings can be interpreted." In 2002, Solórzano and Yosso defined a critical race methodology as a "theoretically grounded approach to research that (a) foregrounds race and racism ... However, it also challenges the separate discourses on race, gender, and class by showing how these three elements intersect to affect the experiences of students of color; (b) challenges the traditional research paradigms, texts, and theories used to explain the experiences of students of color; (c) offers a liberatory or transformative solution to racial, gender, and class subordination; and (d) focuses on the racialized, gendered, and classed experiences of students of color. Furthermore, it ...(c) uses the interdisciplinary knowledge base of ethnic studies, women's studies ... to understand the experiences of students of color" (p. 24).

92. Lynn, M., "Education for the Community."
93. Some of the research that supports this idea follow: Bridges, T. L., "Peace, Love, Unity & Having Fun: Storytelling the Life Histories and Pedagogical Beliefs of African American Male Teachers from the Hip Hop Generation" (Unpublished Dissertation, College Park, MD: University of Maryland, 2009); Gibson, J. R., *Why Black Men Don't Teach and Why We Should: Understanding the Existing African-American Male Teacher Shortage* (New York: KITABU Publishing, LLC, 2009); Kunjufu, J., *Countering the Conspiracy to Destroy Black Boys* (Chicago, IL: African American Images, 1985); Milner, R. H., "A Black Male Teacher's Culturally Responsive Practices," *The Journal of Negro Education* 85, no. 4 (2016): 417–32. https://doi.org/10.7709/jnegroeducation.85.4.0417; and Noguera, P. A., *The Trouble with Black Boys: ... And Other Reflections on Race, Equity, and the Future of Public Education* (San Francisco, CA: Jossey-Bass, 2008).
94. Tafari, "Whose World is This?"
95. Gibson, Why Black Men Don't Teach and Why We Should.
96. Duncan-Andrade, J. M., and E. Morrell, The Art of Critical Pedagogy: Possibilities for Moving From Theory to Practice in Urban Schools (New York: Peter Lang Publishing, Inc., 2008).
97. Nelson, B. G., "The Importance of Men Teachers and Reasons Why There are So Few: A Survey of Members of Naeyc," *MenTeach*, 2002.

98. Bridges, "Peace, Love, Unity & Having Fun."
99. Lynn, M., "Education for the Community."
100. For more information about the PASS program, please visit https://americansportsinstitute.org/programs-services/pass/
101. Duncan-Andrade, J. M., *What a Coach Can Teach a Teacher* (New York: Peter Lang, 2010).
102. All the program-related information on this list has been retrieved from each of the respective websites. Please visit the relevant program site for more details.
103. Though The Teachers' Lounge does not exclusively or predominantly serve Black men teachers, this organization was founded by two Black men educators, cofounders Devin Morris and Jabari Peddie, and this organization was mentioned by one of the gentlemen in this study. Therefore, I included it here.

Printed in the USA
CPSIA information can be obtained
at www.ICGtesting.com
LVHW021254070224
771186LV00081B/2917

9 781942 774914